NO MORE READING FOR JUNK

Dear Readers,

Much like the diet phenomenon *Eat This, Not That*, this series aims to replace some existing practices with approaches that are more effective—healthier, if you will—for our students. We hope to draw attention to practices that have little support in research or professional wisdom and offer alternatives that have greater support. Each text is collaboratively written by authors representing research and practice. Section 1 offers a practitioner's perspective on a practice in need of replacing and helps us understand the challenges, temptations, and misunderstandings that have led us to this ineffective approach. Section 2 provides a researcher's perspective on the lack of research to support the ineffective practice(s) and reviews research supporting better approaches. In Section 3, the author representing a practitioner's perspective gives detailed descriptions of how to implement these better practices. By the end of each book, you will understand both what not to do, and what to do, to improve student learning.

It takes courage to question one's own practice—to shift away from what you may have seen throughout your years in education and toward something new that you may have seen few if any colleagues use. We applaud you for demonstrating that courage and wish you the very best in your journey from this to that.

Best wishes,
— *Nell K. Duke and Ellin Oliver Keene, series editors*

No More Reading for Junk

for Junk

Best Practices for Motivating Readers

BARBARA A. MARINAK

LINDA B. GAMBRELL

HEINEMANN
Portsmouth, NH

Heinemann
361 Hanover Street
Portsmouth, NH 03801–3912
www.heinemann.com

Offices and agents throughout the world

Library of Congress Cataloging-in-Publication Data
Names: Marinak, Barbara A., author. | Gambrell, Linda B., author.
Title: No more reading for junk : best practices for motivating readers /
    Barbara A. Marinak and Linda B. Gambrell.
Description: Portsmouth, NH : Heinemann, [2016] | Series: Not this, but that
    | Includes bibliographical references.
Identifiers: LCCN 2016010144 | ISBN 9780325061573
Subjects: LCSH: Reading (Elementary). | Reading promotion. | Motivation in
    education.
Classification: LCC LB1573 .M3342 2016 | DDC 372.4—dc23

LC record available at https://lccn.loc.gov/2016010144

Series editors: Nell K. Duke *and* Ellin Oliver Keene
Editor: Margaret LaRaia
Production: Vicki Kasabian
Interior design: Suzanne Heiser
Cover design: Lisa A. Fowler
Cover photographs: pinwheel © Comstock/Getty Images/HIP; jacks © Comstock/
            Getty Images/HIP; tickets © Creatas/Getty Images/HIP; dinosaur
            © Issaurinko/iStockphoto.com/Getty Images/HIP; top © malera-
            paso/iStockphoto.com/Getty Images/HIP; pizza © Foodcollection
            .com/Alamy/HIP; stars © Stockdisc/Getty Images/HIP
Typesetter: Valerie Levy, Drawing Board Studios
Manufacturing: Veronica Bennett

Printed in the United States of America on acid-free paper
20   19   18   17   16   VP   1   2   3   4   5

CONTENTS

Introduction Nell K. Duke   vii

SECTION 1   **NOT THIS**

1

We Can't Nurture Intrinsic Reading Motivation Using Rewards/Punishment

Barbara A. Marinak

I Don't Want That Junk Anyway!   2

Rethinking (and Rejecting) a Behaviorist Model   3

Expanding Possibilities   5

Counting Ducks: Rethinking Public Displays of Achievement   6

Tired of Talking Bunnies: Learning About a Passion for Nonfiction   8

Insights from the Underground Book Club   9

I Read Only Dog Books! How a Student's Love of a Book Shaped My Thinking   10

Creating a Motivating Classroom Context for Literacy Learning   11

SECTION 2   **WHY NOT? WHAT WORKS?**

13

What We Know About Reading Motivation, and What It Means for Instruction

Linda B. Gambrell

What's Lost When We Use Rewards and Incentives to Motivate Students to Read   13

Goals of Section 2   15

Why We Say "No More Reading for Junk!"   16

What Theory Tells Us About Motivation to Read   19

Intrinsic Motivation: Getting Students Hooked on the Reading Habit   21

The ARC of Motivation: Access, Relevance, and Choice   22

- *Access: Provide Access to Reading Materials and Opportunities to Read and Discuss Text*   23

- *Relevance: Provide High-Interest, Moderately Challenging, and Authentic Reading Experiences*   26

- *Choice: Provide Opportunities for Students to Self-Select Text and Reading Activities*   30

The *Big* Goal: Supporting Students in Developing Intrinsic Motivation to Read   33

Moving from Understanding to Practice   33

Section 3

34

BUT THAT
Using the ARC of Motivation to Engage All Readers
Barbara A. Marinak and Linda B. Gambrell

The *A* of ARC: Afford *Access* to a Wide Variety of Print   35

- *Recognize Your Super Power!*   37
- *Book Blessing*   38
- *Personal Invitation to Read*   40
- *Picture This!*   42
- *Selecting Books for the Library*   44
- *Engaging Students in Fact Checking*   46

The *R* of ARC: Invite Children into *Relevant* Reading Experiences   48

- *Promote Personal Enjoyment of Reading*   49
- *Celebrate Students' Reading Lives*   51
- *Book Tweets*   54
- *Form Book Clubs*   55
- *Listen Actively*   57
- *Who Knew?*   59

The *C* of ARC: Afford as Much *Choice* as Possible   61

- *Promote Library Values*   62
- *Offer Choice of Teacher Read-Aloud*   63
- *Allow Students to Choose the What, Where, and How*   65
- *Let It Rain! And Other Enticing Book Displays*   68
- *Bridging the Book Divide*   70
- *Representing Reading*   72

Next Steps   75

Afterword Ellin Oliver Keene   77

References   79

INTRODUCTION

NELL K. DUKE

March is Reading Month! In theory, this seems like a great idea: build reading volume and motivation by having a month each year when we celebrate reading, authors, and all things books. But in practice, March is Reading Month often includes practices that not only don't succeed in promoting long-term interest in reading but actually undermine it. How is that possible? Well, often schools, with the best of intentions, provide rewards for reading during the month of March. Depending on the number of minutes or books read, students can earn stickers, small toys, coupons for pizza or other fast-food items, and bigger prizes, such as gift certificates or tickets to a sporting event. The problem is that research suggests that reading for these kinds of incentives not only doesn't encourage reading in the long term, it actually *depresses* motivation to read. In one study, students offered these kinds of incentives were less likely to choose reading as an activity later on than students who received reading-related incentives—in this case, books—or even those who were given no incentives at all.

And who were the authors of this important study? Barbara Marinak and Linda Gambrell (2008)—the authors of this book. Indeed, in this book you have the opportunity to learn from two of the very best. Barbara and Linda bring enormous expertise in how to motivate students to read. Barbara has spent years as a teacher and as an administrator working to develop passionate, lifelong readers. Linda has long worked with teachers and fellow researchers uncovering those approaches and practices that are most promising for fostering reading motivation. I could not be more pleased or proud to feature these educators in this latest installment of the Not This, But That series.

In Section 1, you will learn that early in her career, Barb herself engaged in practices to promote reading motivation that we now recognize as unlikely to be effective (by far my favorite was the time she dressed up as a duck!). Like any of you reading this book, Barbara's heart was in the right place, but she did not yet know of the theory and research that can inform development of reading motivation.

In Section 2, Linda teaches us what research says about fostering reading motivation. You will love the way Linda writes accessibly about a number of research studies related to reading motivation and organizes them into a single model that can powerfully shape our daily practice.

Barbara and Linda team up in Section 3 to describe specific classroom practices you can use to help students want to read and keep reading. Some of these practices are relatively simple to accomplish—such as surveying students about their reading interests or providing an individual student with a book you believe he or she will like; others, such as forming and sustaining book clubs, are more complex but worth every minute. With so many ideas included, I urge you to return to this section again and again as you add practices to your toolkit.

Enjoy reading about reading enjoyment!

SECTION 1
NOT
THIS

We Can't Nurture Intrinsic Reading Motivation Using Rewards/Punishment

BARBARA A. MARINAK[1]

They say the first step in recovery is admitting that you have a problem. Well, I admit it. I spent many years of my career wanting so badly for my students to *love* reading as much as I did that I sometimes resorted to motivation practices that were, shall we say, not helpful. However, that admission puts me a little ahead of the story. I spent several decades in public education in a variety of positions including special educator, reading specialist, reading supervisor, elementary curriculum coordinator, and acting superintendent. Along the way, in each position, I worked tirelessly—though sometimes unwisely—to nurture intrinsic motivation in the students for whom I was responsible. So this is my journey, from an educator with a little knowledge and good intentions to a literacy professional with the same good intentions and more insight. Experiences, studying, working with colleagues,

---

1. And the many wonderful educators she has partnered with through the years.

and, most important, listening to children have taught me a great deal about nurturing intrinsic reading motivation. This initial discussion shares a few of the lessons learned—the most powerful from the children I have been privileged to know.

I Don't Want That Junk Anyway!

While spending time in classrooms recently, I saw student-teacher interaction that gave me pause. Sophia was a bright, inquisitive first grader. Sophie's class was involved in a reading incentive program that included a prize closet. Key chains, Nerf balls, Pez dispensers, and so forth were given for the number of books students read at home. Bags of books went home every day. Parents were required to read with their child

How should we encourage engaged reading?

see Section 3, page 35

and initial a tracking sheet indicating the number of titles read together. If the "right number" were read, based on the tracking sheet, children were invited to pick a prize from the closet. On this particular day, Sophia (and her family) had not achieved the requisite reading for her to pick a prize. Sophia, in all of her spunk, walked up to the prize closet and declared, "I don't want that junk anyway!"

Later conversation with Sophia's teacher revealed that she was a capable, motivated reader with minimal home support. Sophia's situation holds several important lessons. First, we should use reading incentive programs very carefully—if at all. Children should never be punished for minimal reading due to challenging home situations. And, as Sophia reminded us, rewarding reading with "junk" is rarely helpful. In fact, I found myself worrying about Sophia (and other children like her). Could the prize closet "rewards" actually dissuade an already motivated first grader? Sophia's announcement caused me to recall questions from my days in special education.

Rethinking (and Rejecting) a Behaviorist Model

By way of background, my undergraduate training was in deaf education and speech correction. During preservice courses, we were required to assist in a speech and language clinic that served neighborhood children. During these sessions, we rewarded appropriate sound production using token economies. A token economy is behavior modification based on the systematic positive reinforcement of a target behavior. In other words, if a child pronounced a sound correctly, a machine, controlled by me, dispensed a token. The machine was loud and clunky. If he did not pronounce the sound correctly, the machine sat silent. The child collected tokens during the session and could trade them for a larger prize (from a closet) at the end of the session. Sometimes I wondered which was more captivating: the token, the bells and whistles associated with the metal token falling out of the machine, or the time spent with a careful listener.

After obtaining my undergraduate degree, I was certified to work in either speech correction or as a teacher of the hearing impaired. Spending long hours shaping sound production using token economies was not my calling. Becoming a teacher of the hearing impaired seemed much more interesting and challenging. My job was to grow language, literacy, mathematics, science, and social studies. The problem was that even though I left articulation therapy, token economies had not left me.

> **For insights into how to create motivating opportunities**
>
> see Section 2, page 16, and Section 3

Despite soundly rejecting traditional token economy systems (the clunky machines), my early training had (unbeknownst to me at the time) indoctrinated me in behaviorism. I saw motivation as a set of behaviors that I could (and indeed should) shape and reward. So with a pure heart and behaviorist training, I quickly began arranging a reading incentive program in my first classroom. I arranged a complex, arguably convoluted sticker system for reading. My students received stickers for group reading, stickers for independent reading, stickers for at home reading, and stickers for completing reading practice. You get the idea!

Stickers soon became passé. My students were reading, working, and returning their library books, but it didn't take long before they wanted to know what the stickers "got them." "What's the point of the stickers?" a very astute Rhonda asked one day. Good question. Rhonda raised the stakes of the game. What *was* the point of the stickers? What did the sticker get them?

Wanting to keep my students motivated, as measured by their sticker cards, I upped the ante. I began trading scratch and sniffs and smiley faces for larger rewards. My students were soon trading sticker cards for parties and snacks. The interesting observation amid all this frenzy of stickers and food was that my students loved to read. They brought in books to share with each other, couldn't wait to go to the library, and were enthusiastic participants during book discussions. As I was about to discover, other forces were at work. In reality, their reading motivation had little to do with the incentive system I had devised.

So what's a first-year teacher to do? Go to graduate school, of course. In my reading classes at the University of South Carolina, I was introduced to theories other than behaviorism. For the first time, I began to consider an instructional world not governed by tokens and nonsensical rewards. It became clear to me that learning was multidimensional and complex. In other words, the ability to learn and the desire to learn differed for each of my students. And perhaps more important, my graduate work presented a clear message: I mattered. As the teacher, what I did or did not do had a significant impact on my students' ability and willingness to risk, persevere through challenges, and take pride in their accomplishments. Much to think about!

Though it was difficult to abandon my incentive program (the roots of behaviorism ran deep), I became convinced that stickers had nothing to do with the reading motivation I saw. The first hint of this was the realization that forgetting stickers didn't matter but cutting short book discussion did. I came to understand that if my students were going to assume responsibility for reading, I had to relinquish control. In doing so, what they valued became clear. Affording my students choice, surrounding them with books, reading aloud, and encouraging conversations were the authentic and enduring practices that would most likely nurture intrinsic reading motivation.

It is time for all of us to rethink prize closets, treasure chests, and other caches of tangible rewards. Though children might like a key chain, Nerf ball, or pizza, these incentives are so far removed from reading that they will do little to nurture intrinsic motivation. As we will discuss in Sections 2 and 3, prize closets can be closed and replaced with engaging experiences that grow autonomy and risk taking. Pizza and Pez dispensers are short lived, but confident, empowered readers are likely to remain motivated for life.

Section 2 will provide the background on why these approaches work.

Section 3 will give you details on how to make these ideas work in your classroom.

Expanding Possibilities

I was a precocious reader when I was young, but not because my parents "taught" me to read. Instead, they did all the right stuff. They read aloud constantly, provided lots of print in the house, and shared stories around the dinner table. In fact, I could read before I went to kindergarten. Sounds good—right? Not so much. In those days, kindergarten was for singing, napping, and eating snacks. Kind of deadly for an active five-year-old! It was the job of the first-grade teacher to "teach" us to read. This responsibility was strictly designated and carefully guarded. So too was the library. There was a K–2 section and an area for older readers. Needless to say, by the time I was in second grade, I had read most everything in my section. I was bored, and bored kids either get in trouble or someone recognizes their need for challenge. One day, while wandering aimlessly among the picture books, I heard a voice behind me say, rather sternly, "Barbara!" I remember thinking, "Well, it's off to the principal's office . . . again!" Not so. Mrs. Williams, the school librarian, told me it was time to visit the section of the library reserved for students in grades 3–6. I couldn't believe my ears, and before long, *Harriet the Spy* (Fitzhugh 1964) was in my hand. To this day, I believe Mrs. Williams saved my reading life. She gave me access to a world of books I had only glanced at from afar. Not long after I was invited to this previously restricted section, the school principal realized that the library should be opened up for everyone. And that is how it remained until recently.

Unfortunately, the notion of restricting access to books in the library is back with a vengeance. Several reading programs suggest that children read books only "on their level." I have always been befuddled by that phrase. I am not exactly sure what it means because all children have multiple reading levels, depending upon experience, interests, background knowledge, passion, and so on. Some programs attempt to control all reading at school and well beyond the walls of the classroom. This is done by "dotting" the school library. Dotting entails placing small colored circles on books indicating the discrete levels children are permitted to select from. In other words, children on an orange level can borrow only orange-dotted books. Where is Mrs. Williams when you need her? Based on Benjamin Franklin's vision, the library is a sacred sanctuary where readers should have the freedom to explore, browse, and change their minds unencumbered by their "level."

Counting Ducks: Rethinking Public Displays of Achievement

This next story is an example of good intentions gone wrong. During my school district days I had a building principal who believed in reading incentive programs. After much wrangling, I talked him out of the pizza program and all things "junk." We agreed the program should involve time spent reading (versus the number of books) and count all reading time (in and out of school) so as not to punish students with busy or distracted families. And the prize would be a movie night with children, teachers, and their families.

Our first schoolwide theme was "Duck Away with a Book." We launched the program in September, and it concluded in early spring after a long and snowy winter. Yours truly dressed up in a duck costume and greeted the kids as they came off the school bus. I made a total fool of myself, quacking and flapping my way through the buses, parking lot, and every classroom. The kids were hysterical! I got their attention for sure. The buzz (or quack) was audible throughout the building. They couldn't wait for the duck to visit. Was there excitement? Absolutely! Did the duck suit nurture intrinsic motivation to read? Probably not. The duck suit was intended as a spark: We were hoping to ignite curiosity and engagement. We planned to feed that fire through months of encouragement, notes home, and individual conversations. What we didn't realize is how much our "cute" launch diminished the true accomplishments of student reading.

In an attempt to celebrate all the reading the students did, we posted a hand-cut duck in the school hallway for every fifteen minutes of time spent reading. School volunteers snipped hundreds of ducks! Friday nights were spent with pizza and ladders as teachers hung ducks in the hallway, each with a child's name. The more children read, the more ducks appeared. The building was developing camaraderie around reading. Or so we thought. Then we started listening to the children. We heard murmurs like "Well, Matthew has more ducks than me" and "I will never have as many ducks as Jena." We even heard comments like "I don't like looking at the ducks any more," sadly from highly motivated children. Despite our best intentions, we had created what some refer to as "public displays of humiliation." The celebration had turned into a competition. The focus became counting and comparing versus loving reading. Lesson learned.

Public displays of achievement must be approached with great caution. Celebrating reading is more effective when offered individually and based on individual goals and interests. We are much less likely to erode intrinsic motivation in those who already love to read when we plan celebratory conversations with the important people in a child's life: teacher, family, coach, principal, and so on. In reality, the ducks did little more than make our custodians cranky—the upper halls had to be repainted thanks to extra-sticky masking tape. Those ducks didn't come down easily!

Tired of Talking Bunnies: Learning About a Passion for Nonfiction

Six-year-old Matthew taught me a valuable lesson about reading motivation. Matthew was one of three gifted children I had the pleasure of working with several years ago. My job seemed easy—enrich and challenge an already motivated group of precocious readers. I met with the children three times a week to share books. Our book collection, like many still are today, was predominately fiction. Matthew and his friends were devouring the series short chapter books, and I was soon out of options. I decided to purchase more challenging chapter books, and an array of brand-new titles greeted the group on their next visit. Everyone seemed pleased except Matthew. Before I could ask, he announced his displeasure. "Dr. M., I'm pretty tired of talking bunnies!" Message received. When I inquired, Matthew described his preferences in great detail. "I want to learn about what happens inside an egg before the chicken hatches, and then I want to teach it to the rest of the class." The group quickly agreed, and our embryology unit began. Each of the students selected a different bird, did research using a wide variety of texts, and created big books for their class lessons. They did an amazing job!

In reflecting on this experience with the first-grade teachers and digging into the research, we realized that Matthew had taught us some important lessons about reading motivation. First, our book collection needed balance. We needed to offer more nonfiction in a wide variety of forms including books, magazines, and web-based articles. Second, we had to stop assuming we knew what children wanted to read. We dedicated ourselves to asking and listening carefully because not all students were as forthright as Matthew. Many were quietly compliant. They read whatever we decided without complaint. However, as we admitted to ourselves, compliant readers are not necessarily motivated readers. In fact, most probably are not. Last, and perhaps most important, Matthew was requesting relevant reading. He wanted to read for a purpose. He wanted to do something meaningful with his new knowledge. This was a critical lesson for us. We can nurture intrinsic reading motivation by planning instruction with relevance in mind.

Insights from the Underground Book Club

A group of students whispering in the hall one day taught me another important lesson about reading motivation: the power of underground book clubs. An underground book club is a group of children reading something they perceive to be "not school." Places to discover your underground book clubs are those areas where kids have quiet conversations such as the cafeteria and playground or while standing in various lines.

We happened upon one while walking by students' lockers. We saw several students talking quietly with backpacks in hand. We heard whispers like, "If you bring me 42, I'll give you 38." What in the world were they talking about? Turns out, it was *Goosebumps* (Stine 1992–1997). This series of semi-scary books was not available at school, so the students created their own lending library. Brilliant! Not wanting to spoil the clandestine excitement, we weren't sure what to do. Should we ask them about the books, or just ignore it? We decided to venture in.

Remarkable things came from that conversation. The students were anxious to talk about the series and why they loved it. They "kind of"

To learn more about the power of peers to sustain reading motivation

see Section 2, page 24, and Section 3, page 55

understood why the books were not available at school. "Not great literature," offered one young man. "But reading fun books is OK, isn't it?" No doubt about it! The underground book club led to building discussions about honoring all print during independent reading time. It caused us to ask about all the "not school" reading our students were doing. And, wow, did they love that we asked! The result? *Goosebumps* came out of the shadows, as did list books, joke books, magazines, and the sports page from the local newspaper.

I Read Only Dog Books! How a Student's Love of a Book Shaped My Thinking

In a passionate pronouncement, a student named Mackenzie changed my thinking forever. Perhaps the most challenging students to motivate are our struggling readers, and rightly so. For them, reading is hard and probably has been for a long time. However, some of the most poignant lessons we learned came from students who struggled the most. If we have any hope of nurturing intrinsic reading motivation, we need to meet these children where they are. Take time to listen, find text about their passions, and help them discover new ones! It's not hard to do. Print is available about most any subject they might select. We have found endless reading material about snakes, motorcycles, sports teams, Indiana Jones—you name it. Meeting them where they are builds respect about reading. Once trust is established, it is easy to link a student's initial interests to new topics or genres. I must admit, however, we were challenged by one student. Mackenzie was a student with autistic spectrum disorder. Comprehension was a struggle, and change was hard. We were delighted when she announced early on, "I read only dog books!" Not a problem, we thought. There are lots of dog books available. Not exactly. What Mackenzie meant was, I read only *this* dog book. And that book was 2011's *Dog Heroes of September 11th: A Tribute to America's Search and Rescue Dogs* by Nona Kilgore Bauer (Marinak, Gambrell, and Malloy 2013). She wanted to read it over and over again. What choice did we have? Luckily, this oversized, beautifully photographed text, which honors the dogs who participated in the 9/11 rescues, was rich with possibilities. We created numerous lessons from the text and found other books and articles about rescue dogs. And once we met Mackenzie where she was, she was willing to try a few titles we suggested. Before long, she discovered she could read and enjoy nonfiction about whales, dolphins, and otters. But, to this day, *Dog Heroes of September 11th: A Tribute to America's Search and Rescue Dogs* remains her favorite. It will most likely never leave her backpack, and that is just fine.

Mackenzie taught us never to assume. She reminded us to listen carefully. Sometimes nurturing intrinsic motivation means we need to meet students where they are.

Creating a Motivating Classroom Context for Literacy Learning

We have learned many lessons through the years, from the research, each other, and, most important, from our students. These lessons inform our practice. Our goal is to have students who can read, who choose to read, and who enjoy reading a variety of text. Students who enjoy reading and are motivated to read are likely to choose to read more often than students who do not enjoy reading. And, the more students read, the better readers they become. Reading achievement has been linked to a better and more productive academic, social, and civic life. We really don't need to be convinced that reading is a good thing for our students. The larger question is, how do we help out students develop the reading habit?

In this section, I have shared my journey and concerns over the years about how to effectively motivate all students to read. This journey is clearly nomadic. I don't expect to ever arrive. I continue to teach, read research, and learn from colleagues about effective motivation strategies and techniques.

In the next section, Linda will focus on what research reveals about creating a classroom context that nurtures reading motivation and literacy learning. She provides a research-based context for what we call the ARC of motivation. The ARC represents: *access*, *relevance*, and *choice*. Then in Section 3 we will share ARC strategies and techniques that invite you to start thinking differently about how you can foster reading motivation in your classroom!

WHY NOT? WHAT WORKS?

What We Know About Reading Motivation, and What It Means for Instruction

LINDA B. GAMBRELL

What's Lost When We Use Rewards and Incentives to Motivate Students to Read

In the town of Pageville, the Principal of Hobbit Elementary School places a high value on reading and wanted to motivate the students to spend more time reading. In September, he called all the students into the assembly room and announced a reading challenge: "If Pageville Elementary students read 1,000 books before the end of the school year I will spend an entire day on the roof of the school." The three hundred K–6 students at Pageville were up to the challenge! Students read, teachers recorded the books completed, and, sure enough, on May 1, the principal spent the day on the roof, sitting in his favorite chair that had also been hoisted to the roof!

While Pageville is an imaginary town, this story is not. The "principal on the roof" is an incentive that many schools have used, in one variation or another, in an effort to increase students' motivation to read. In this book we take a careful and thoughtful look at the research base for practices that promote motivation to read and those that do not. While there are no studies that suggest that the "principal on the roof" results in increased motivation to read, it probably does encourage some students to spend time reading. The major concern, however, is whether this practice results in any long-term impact on students' motivation to read and, in particular, does it increase reading motivation for those students who struggle with literacy learning. Activities such as "principal on the roof" bring to the forefront the issue of whether there is educational value in using incentives and rewards to promote reading motivation.

Let's examine the "principal on the roof" event in light of what research tells us about motivating students to read. Studies indicate that the "principal on the roof" will most likely not be effective in nurturing students' motivation to read for several reasons. First, the reward of seeing the principal sitting on the roof is too far removed (by weeks and perhaps months) from the actual act of reading. Research indicates that when rewarding a behavior in an attempt to foster motivation, the presentation of the reward must be immediate. Students value the reward less the longer they have to wait. In addition, it is important to note that even if the reward of the principal sitting on the roof were more immediate, due to the extrinsic nature of the incentive, the effects would be short lived (Fryer et al. 2012).

In addition, incentives such as the "principal on the roof" do not nurture motivation because they are not closely related, or proximal, to the desired behavior (reading). Having a principal engage in a humorous act like sitting on the roof, while entertaining and perhaps temporarily interesting, is not directly related to the desired behavior of reading. In other words, if students who are not motivated to read participate in this activity, their reading engagement is most likely to be temporary and only for the purpose of seeing the principal on the roof—not because they have become more motivated to read (Marinak and Gambrell 2008).

Goals of Section 2

Section 2 of this book will form the link between the important issues raised in Section 1 and the research-based motivational strategies and techniques that will be described in Section 3. Teachers want their students to be intrinsically motivated to read—to choose to read for personal pleasure and information. Teachers recognize the importance of being able to read and know that reading is the gateway to both academic and personal success. Because we, as educators, know the value and importance of reading, we want our students to be interested and excited about reading. Again, we want our students to be intrinsically motivated to read, rather than to be dependent upon extrinsic incentives and rewards. The major goals of this section are to describe the research evidence that "reading for junk" is counterproductive, provide an overview of what theory and research tell us about motivation to read, and make research-based recommendations for creating classroom contexts that support the development of intrinsic reading motivation.

Intrinsic Motivation to Read

Self-generated interest in reading that brings pleasure that is inherent in engaging in reading tasks and activities.

Extrinsic Motivation to Read

Externally oriented interest in reading based on rewards and incentives.

Why We Say "No More Reading for Junk!"

Decades of research clearly indicate that extrinsic rewards can actually undermine intrinsic reading motivation. One of the reasons for this is that every extrinsic reward carries with it the potential to either control or inform. If the reward informs, it can result in greater feelings of competence and foster intrinsic motivation (for example, the teacher provides feedback that informs such as, "You read that passage with great expression!"). If, however, the reward is seen as controlling, the result can be an erosion of intrinsic motivation (for example, "You will get a sticker for every book you read."). Though well intentioned, extrinsic incentives and rewards can actually serve to undermine the desired effect (Schunk, Pintrich, and Meece 2008).

> **Section 1 contains examples of practices that can erode intrinsic motivation.**

Cameron and Pierce (1994) conducted a large meta-analysis of the research on rewards and concluded that extrinsic rewards do not necessarily have a positive or negative impact on intrinsic motivation with respect to nurturing intrinsic reading motivation, attitude, time on task, and performance. Studies on extrinsic rewards, however, have shown mixed results. A number of studies have shown that, under certain conditions, extrinsic rewards can enhance motivation. In these studies, students who were given an incentive (promised a reward for certain behavior) showed an increase in intrinsic motivation compared to students who were not offered an incentive (Brennan and Glover 1980; Karnoil and Ross 1977). On the other hand, other researchers have reported a negative effect on intrinsic motivation when incentives were promised for a specified level of performance (Deci 1975; Lepper, Greene, and Nisbett 1973). So, at best, the research on the use of rewards is "fuzzy." The work that is perhaps the most informative on this issue is the study by Deci and his colleagues that suggests that if you reward a student who enjoys reading with an extrinsic reward (such as points, food, or money), the student may choose to read less frequently once the incentive is discontinued (Deci et al. 1991). The concern then is that extrinsic rewards may have a detrimental effect on the intrinsic motivation to read, particularly for those students who are already intrinsically motivated to read.

Interesting evidence also suggests that individuals are motivated by the reward itself (Deci 1975). For example, if we are paid to do a task such as reading, it may result in a decrease in our desire to read; however, being paid may be very effective in motivating an individual to make money. In other words, we tend to view the "reward" as desirable and valuable. Therefore, if we want to develop the intrinsic desire to read, books and extra time to read are probably the most effective rewards.

We do have to acknowledge that incentives and rewards are a part of everyday life. For example, we are rewarded with a paycheck for the work we do, we promise ourselves a "celebration" dinner when we've lost ten pounds, or we shop at the same supermarket each week to get points for a Thanksgiving turkey. None of these "rewards" are necessarily bad or negative. What the research strongly suggests, however, is that we must be very thoughtful about how and when we use rewards.

My observations in the classroom of a truly outstanding teacher influenced my thinking about the role of rewards in motivating students to learn. In this classroom the teacher used primarily intangible extrinsic rewards, along with some tangible rewards that were clearly related to academics, to motivate her students to engage in learning. For example, after a reading skill group where all children were able to demonstrate mastery, she rewarded the students with ten extra minutes of free reading time. Following a reading lesson using a text about space travel, she rewarded the students with the opportunity to read a more challenging text on the same topic for homework, if they chose to do so. Every child in the reading group eagerly chose to take home the more challenging text as a reading assignment. After another whole-class lesson, the teacher rewarded the class by saying, "You all did such great work . . . I'm going to read two chapters to you during teacher read-aloud time today."

What this teacher did was to demonstrate every day the value of reading and other academic tasks. Also, note that her rewards required students to engage in more work related to her learning objective and the "rewards" in her classroom almost always required the students to engage in more academic learning. In this classroom the students valued the rewards, and the rewards were more academic work! By using academic tasks as rewards, this teacher demonstrated that these kinds of tasks and activities are valued in this classroom. When candy or stickers are given as rewards, the message is that candy and stickers are valued. Rewarding students with opportunities to engage in more challenging academic tasks sends a clear message that literacy learning is valued.

My observations in the classroom of this outstanding teacher led me to develop the "reward proximity hypothesis." This hypothesis posits that the closer the reward (books, reading time, etc.) to the desired behavior (engaging in independent reading), the greater the likelihood that intrinsic motivation will increase (Gambrell and Marinak 1997).

In a study designed to explore the reward proximity hypothesis, elementary students were asked to read books in order to select good books for the school library. One group of students received books as rewards, one group received small tokens (rings, small cars, erasers, etc.), and a control group received no reward. The students who were rewarded with books and the no-reward group chose reading as a follow-up activity more often than students who were given small tokens as a reward (Marinak and Gambrell 2008). Clearly, in this study the token reward had an undermining effect on motivation to read, while intrinsic motivation was not diminished when students received books as a reward. These results support the notion that if rewards are used, they should always be closely related to the desired behavior—reading!

Creating a classroom climate that nurtures and supports the development of intrinsic motivation to read should be a high priority. It is the teacher who is central to creating a classroom environment that inspires students to be engaged and motivated literacy learners (Wayne and

Youngs 2003). Effective teachers promote intrinsic motivation to engage in reading and other literacy tasks in a variety of ways, including the way they establish a classroom environment that provides a rich array of reading materials, tasks, and activities that are relevant to students' interests and opportunities for choice.

For ideas to nurture intrinsic reading motivation

see Section 3, page 68

What Theory Tells Us About Motivation to Read

The research on motivation to read is informed by a number of theories. Understanding these theories of motivation can help you make good choices about how to motivate your students to read. Motivation to read is defined as the likelihood of engaging in a reading task and persisting in the activity despite challenges. This definition is based on decades of research by behavioral, humanistic, cognitive, and social-cognitive psychologists. In the early twentieth century, behavioral psychologists maintained that our motivations grow from interactions with our environment, meaning that we are driven by things we want to attain (e.g., rewards, incentives) or avoid (e.g., unpleasant consequences) (Skinner 1953; Thorndike 1910; Watson 1913). When students read solely for the purpose of receiving rewards (such as points, toys, or food), they are responding to an environment that treats reading as something that is externally controlled. Many educators question both the quality of students' interactions with text when using these methods, as well as the value of these extrinsic motivators as a means of encouraging students to read for the intrinsic purposes of pleasure and gaining information (Lepper, Greene, and Nisbett 1973; Mallette, Henk, and Melnick 2004).

In keeping with humanistic and cognitive psychology, Deci and Ryan (1985) describe their self-determination theory as the need to experience control in our lives. Students who feel that they have some control over their learning have been found to engage more meaningfully with literacy tasks (Turner 1995) and to be willing to undertake greater challenges in learning (Csikszentmihalyi 1990).

Goal theory describes how and why students set goals for achievement (Ames 1992; Dweck and Leggett 1988). Task goals are described as a desire for personal improvement and mastery of a skill, while ability goals focus on one's performance in relation to others. Broadly related to the developing understanding of goal theory are the constructs of intrinsic and extrinsic motivation (Lepper, Greene, and Nisbett 1973). Intrinsic motivation can be described as interest in an activity that brings a pleasure that is inherent in engaging in the activity itself—for example, finishing a book because you can't wait to find out what happens. Describing a heightened form of intrinsic involvement, Csikszentmihalyi (1990) describes the experience of being totally absorbed in an activity, such as reading a great book, as "flow." In the "flow" experience one is so intrinsically motivated that one loses the perception of place or of time passing.

A contemporary view of motivation is expressed by the social-cognitive theory that suggests that we are driven by what we think of ourselves and the task presented. The expectancy-value theory suggests that an individual's perception of potential success (expectancy) in performing a task and the perceived value attributed to the activity are determinants of the person's willingness to engage in achievement behaviors (Eccles et al. 1983). Perceptions of expectancy are influenced by the individual's sense of competence in completing a task successfully, while perceptions of value are influenced by the importance and usefulness of the task (Bandura 1977; Eccles et al. 1983).

For ideas to personally invite students into reading

see Section 3, page 40

This theory suggests that scaffolding tasks and activities so that students have increasing success at challenging literacy tasks will increase students' feelings of competence and motivation to read. Likewise, helping students see the value and importance of reading will also increase motivation to read.

Intrinsic Motivation: Getting Students Hooked on the Reading Habit

Intrinsic reading motivation refers to a student's inner desire to engage in reading, regardless of whether there is an incentive or reward for doing so. For example, an intrinsically motivated student will choose to read during free time at school or over the summer holiday. On the other hand, extrinsic reading motivation refers to students who engage in reading because of an incentive or reward—for example, a student is told that she will receive a prize, such as a bag of candy or a toy car, if she reads for ten minutes a day for a week. A study by Wigfield and Guthrie (1995) revealed that there were a number of intrinsic and extrinsic motivational factors related to the amount of time students spent reading, including reading proficiency, curiosity, involvement, recognition, and grades. Most important, Wigfield and Guthrie concluded that intrinsic motivations for reading were more strongly related to time spent reading than extrinsic motivations. Students are more likely to choose to read and intrinsic motivation is nurtured when students are given ample time and opportunity to read.

A number of studies have documented that the amount and breadth of reading that students do is the single largest factor contributing to reading achievement (Cunningham and Stanovich 1998; Guthrie and Humenick 2004). In addition, there is evidence that motivation to read in the elementary and middle school years is related to reading achievement, with more proficient readers being more motivated and less proficient readers being less motivated (McKenna 2001; McKenna, Kear, and Ellsworth 1995; Petscher 2010). The relationship between reading motivation and reading achievement is complex and, according to McKenna et al. (2012), possibly reciprocal, with poor readers experiencing frustrations that result in decreased motivation, "which in turn inhibit voluntary reading, which consequently constrains growth in proficiency" (287).

We know that some students expend great time and effort on academic tasks such as reading, while other students do not. One of the lingering questions is why different students expend different amounts of time and effort on such tasks. Such differences are often explained as motivational in nature: Some students are more highly motivated to read than others. During the past decade there has been increasing interest in classroom factors that are specifically associated with reading motivation. Research indicates that classroom environments that provide access to a variety of reading materials, reading activities that are relevant, and opportunities for student choice are more likely to nurture reading engagement and achievement (Anderman and Midgley 1992; Gambrell 2011; Guthrie, Wigfield, and VonSecker 2000).

The ARC of Motivation: Access, Relevance, and Choice

How do we create a classroom environment that supports and nurtures intrinsic motivation to read? Classroom instruction that provides students with decoding and comprehension skills and strategies is necessary but not sufficient. We believe that motivation is central to reading development, and if students are not motivated to read, they will never reach their full literacy potential. It is simply not enough to teach our students to read; we want them to leave our classrooms with the intrinsic motivation to read for pleasure and for information and to read widely and deeply across a wide array of genres.

Intrinsic motivation to read has been associated with a number of desirable outcomes including higher reading achievement, deeper cognitive processing, greater conceptual understanding, and willingness to persevere (Hidi 1990; Tobias 1994). In this section we will briefly review research that focuses on classroom practices that hold promise for increasing students' intrinsic motivation to read. Studies conducted over the past two decades reveal some essential elements for creating classroom contexts that nurture intrinsic motivation to read. We refer to these elements as the ARC of motivation: Access,

Relevance, and Choice (ARC). As Figure 2–1 illustrates, these elements are not discrete to a particular reading task, activity, strategy, or technique; rather, they overlap in important ways.

Figure 2–1 ARC of Motivation

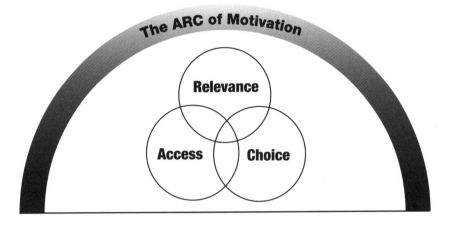

Access: Provide Access to Reading Materials and Opportunities to Read and Discuss Text

Access refers to having a classroom with a wide variety of reading materials available for students, as well as time and opportunities for students to read and talk about what they are reading. If we want students to be motivated readers, we must create a classroom context that is text-rich and celebrates the joy and value of reading. In classrooms that are text-rich, teachers display books to attract students' attention and interest, select interesting and informative books to read aloud, and introduce new books as they are added to the classroom library.

Reading Materials. A number of studies have documented that when students have classrooms that are rich in reading materials, motivation to read is high (Guthrie and McCann 1997; Neuman and Celano 2001). Being surrounded by an abundance of high-quality, high-interest reading materials is critical to the development of reading motivation.

Availability of books and other reading materials encourages students to engage in reading in a voluntary and sustained manner. One caveat worth noting with regard to access to reading materials is that it is not just having books and other reading materials available that is important—rather, it is how the materials are made accessible to students and what teachers do to promote engagement with books and other reading materials. We know, for example, that when books are displayed or featured in some way by the teacher that students gravitate toward them (Morrow 1982; Morrow 1990). It is also true that students want to reread books that the teacher has read aloud. Having books available and having a teacher who promotes reading in interesting and exciting ways creates a motivating context for literacy learning.

Classrooms should provide a wide range of reading choices for students that reflect their interests and preferences: narrative and informational texts, resource and reference books, poetry, newspapers, magazines, and, of course, access to the Internet and other forms of digital print. Providing a variety of reading materials that reflects authentic forms of text communicates to students that reading is a worthwhile and valuable activity and sets the stage for students to develop the reading habit.

Daily Classroom Reading Time. Students are more motivated to read when they have ample opportunities to engage in sustained reading. According to Hiebert (2009), students' lack of motivation to read can be traced to an insufficient amount of time spent reading in classrooms. Classrooms where students have ample time and opportunities to engage in sustained reading provide the foundation needed to support them in becoming engaged and proficient readers. Studies have documented that time spent reading is associated with both reading proficiency and intrinsic motivation to read (Allington and McGill-Franzen 2003; Mizelle 1997; Taylor, Frye, and Maruyama 1990).

In a study of classrooms where at least ninety minutes was devoted to reading/language arts instruction, Brenner, Hiebert, and Tompkins

(2010) found that students spent an average of only eighteen minutes actually engaged in the sustained reading of text. Foorman et al. (2006) examined time allocation during reading instruction in first- and second-grade classrooms and found that the amount of time provided for reading was associated with growth in reading proficiency. In this study, only time devoted to text reading significantly explained gains on posttest reading measures, including word reading, decoding, and passage comprehension. No other time-allocation factors, including time spent on word, alphabetic, or phonemic awareness instruction, contributed to reading growth. Other studies have investigated the effects of time spent reading on reading achievement. In a study of reading interventions, Allington (2011) found that in the most successful interventions, two-thirds of student time was spent on reading and rereading. Taylor, Frye, and Maruyama (1990) reported that time spent reading in school was highly correlated with reading achievement. In a subsequent study, Guthrie et al. (1999) found that the amount of time spent reading predicted reading comprehension.

What is the "just-right" amount of independent time that students need? According to Miller and Moss (2013), there is no clear-cut answer, but the amount of time needed may depend on reader proficiency. In a study of children in grades 3–5, Wu and Samuels (2004) compared a group of students who read independently for fifteen minutes a day to a group that read independently for forty minutes a day. Students read books that were appropriate to their reading ability. In this study, good readers benefited more from the forty-minute reading time than the poor readers, while poor readers benefited more from the fifteen-minute reading time. In other words, the shorter time allotment was more effective for the poorer readers, while the longer time allotments helped the good readers. This finding suggests that different time allocations should be provided for students at different ages and stages of proficiency. Most important, if we want students to be motivated to read independently, then we have to "make it a practice that happens during classroom time" (Miller and Moss 2013).

Daily Classroom Time for Talking About Text. Talking about text includes reading together with others, borrowing and sharing books, and talking with peers about books in class. Time to talk about text supports motivation in a variety of ways (Guthrie, Wigfield, and Von Secker 2000; Turner and Paris 1995). First, peer comments can pique a student's curiosity. Second, talking with others promotes student interest and engagement. A number of studies indicate that instruction that incorporates talk about text increases students' motivation to read and reading comprehension achievement (Gambrell et al. 2011; Guthrie, McRae, and Klauda 2007; Ng et al. 1998).

The skills students learn through talking about what they have read are *crossover skills* because they are used in talking, reading, and writing to the benefit of all three (Morrow, Roskos, and Gambrell 2015). A few of the most essential skills are making predictions, asking and answering questions, and telling and retelling stories and information. Providing tasks and activities that provide students with opportunities to talk about text will support both reading proficiency and motivation.

Relevance: Provide High-Interest, Moderately Challenging, and Authentic Reading Experiences

One way to make reading more relevant for students is to focus on high-interest and authentic activities. Research suggests that high-interest texts and activities reflect what the student finds both appealing and challenging (Fulmer and Frijters 2011). Authentic reading activities are more like those found in the "real" world, such as reading a letter from a pen pal, as opposed to school-like activities, such as completing worksheets (Purcell-Gates 2002).

Match Students with High-Interest Texts. When students find a book that they are interested in reading, they are likely to be more inclined to read that book. This is a common-sense notion that is supported by research on the role of interest in reading development

(Hidi 1990). Tapping in to what students are interested in reading and building on that interest is a powerful factor in motivating students to read. When students have access to engaging reading materials, they read with greater attention, concentration, and willingness to sustain their reading (Krapp, Hidi, and Renninger 1992).

Students' reading interests are highly individual. Factors such as age, gender, home environment, classroom environment, and academic ability are a few of the factors that influence students' reading preferences. Moss and Young (2010) suggest three techniques to help determine an individual student's interests. First, observe, note, and record students' interests as they participate in various classroom reading tasks and activities. Second, engage in informal discussions with students, parents, peers, and others to help identify particular areas of interest both in and out of school. Third, use interest inventories to learn about student interests. (See Moss and Young [2010, 57] for an example of a Reading Interest Survey.)

Provide Moderately Challenging Reading Texts and Activities.

Another feature of motivating reading activities is that they advance, rather than overwhelm, the reader (Turner 1995). If the text is too difficult, the reader is more likely to give up. On the other hand, if the text is too easy, the reader is more likely to become bored. The most motivating reading texts and activities are moderately challenging, where the student must put forth some effort—but with effort comes some level of success. Success with challenging reading tasks provides students with evidence of accomplishment, resulting in increased feelings of competence and increased motivation (Schunk 1989; Schunk and Zimmerman 1997). Research indicates that students who *believe* that they are capable and competent readers are more likely to outperform those who do not hold such beliefs (Paris and Oka 1986; Schunk 1989; Schunk and Zimmerman 1997).

Building on students' interests has been shown to promote success and increased comprehension of moderately challenging text. A recent

For examples of Barb's movement toward more authentic reading opportunities

see Section 1

study conducted by Fulmer and Frijters (2011) provides some insights about the important role of topic interest when students are reading challenging materials. They investigated students' motivation while reading excessively challenging text. They found that high-topic interest served as a buffer in that students were able to read and comprehend challenging text better when the text reflected a topic of high personal interest. Students who read a text they rated as *most personally interested* reported higher interest and enjoyment and lower ratings of attributions of difficulty and were almost twice as likely to persist with the reading. This research lends support to the notion that a challenging text may be less problematic if students are personally interested in its topic.

Provide Authentic "Real-World" Reading Text and Activities.
Authentic reading experiences are analogous to those that are encountered in the day-to-day lives of people, as opposed to typical classroom activities such as answering teacher-posed questions and completing worksheets. Authentic reading tasks acknowledge and play into students' interest in doing things that are "real life."

Purcell-Gates, Duke, and Martineau (2007) conducted a study of authentic literacy activities—those that involve meaningful, purposeful, and functional experiences that motivate and engage students—and found that teachers who included more authentic literacy activities had students who showed higher growth in reading comprehension. They defined authentic reading activities as those that replicate or reflect reading that occurs in the lives of people outside of a learning-to-read context and purpose.

Gambrell and colleagues (2011) conducted a year-long study of authentic reading, writing, and discussion tasks in third-, fourth-, and fifth-grade classrooms. In this study, reading, writing, and discussion were examined within the context of a pen pal project that engaged students in authentic literacy tasks. Throughout the year, students and adult pen pals read the same high-quality children's books and exchanged letters about the books. The adult pen pals encouraged students to engage in close reading of the text by posing higher-order questions such as "Let me know what you think about . . ." or "I'll be interested to know if you agree with . . ." Students participated in at least two small-group discussions of each book. The small-group discussions were purposeful and authentic because the "talk" focused on issues and questions raised by the adult pen pal. The major finding from this study was that there was a statistically significant increase in student's literacy motivation over the course of the school year. Findings integrated across quantitative and qualitative data sources suggested that authentic literacy tasks have the potential to support and sustain students' literacy motivation.

A number of researchers believe that the concept of moving everyday life experiences into the classroom is essential to the process of reading development (Brophy 2008; Brown, Collins, and Duguid 1989; Neuman and Roskos 1997). On the other hand, some might argue that incorporating truly authentic reading experiences in the classroom is rarely possible. Therefore, we think it is more realistic to consider authentic reading tasks and activities on a continuum from "less authentic" to "more authentic," always with the goal of increasing the real-life nature of the reading experience.

Purcell-Gates (1996, 2002) proposed two criteria for determining the authenticity of literacy tasks: text and purpose. First, does the text read by the student exist outside of a learning-to-read context? For example, a worksheet on animals that hibernate would not be an authentic text, while a book from the library on creatures that hibernate would be. Second, are the purposes for which the text is read the same as that for which it is used outside of the classroom context? For example, having students answer teacher-posed questions about a text would be "less authentic," while a peer-led, small-group discussion would be "more authentic" because readers often participate in book club discussions in the real world. To judge the authenticity of a reading activity, Duke et al. (2006) suggest that teachers look at both *text* and *purpose*. They developed a three-point scale that teachers can use to rate the degree to which the text and purpose of the reading activity mirrors real-life reading activities (see Duke et al. 2006, 347).

Choice: Provide Opportunities for Students to Self-Select Text and Reading Activities

For many years psychologists have contended that providing choice will increase an individual's sense of personal control (Rotter 1966) and intrinsic motivation (Deci and Ryan 1985). Research indicates that students are more motivated to read when they have opportunities to self-select materials for reading and make choices about their reading tasks and activities (Cambourne 1995; Guthrie et al. 1999; Schunk and Zimmerman 1997; Turner 1995).

Text Choice. When students are allowed to choose what they read, research indicates that they engage in reading more often (Reynolds and Symons 2001), understand more of what they read (Guthrie and Humenick 2004), and are more likely to continue reading (Ainley, Hidi, and Berndorff 2002; Allington, Gabriel, and Billen 2012). Having students self-select what they want to read allows them to focus on texts that are of high-interest to them. Research supports the notion that the texts that students find most interesting are those they have selected for their own reasons and purposes (Palmer, Codling, and Gambrell 1994; Pressley 2007). Schiefele's (1991) research revealed that students who were allowed and encouraged to choose their own reading materials expended more effort in learning and understanding the material they read.

A study conducted by Wiesendanger and Birlem (1984) analyzed eleven research studies on self-selected reading and reported that nine of these studies presented evidence that students were more motivated to read as a result of participating in self-selected reading. In a more recent study Guthrie, McRae, and Klauda (2007) explored fourth-grade students' motivation and reading comprehension growth and reported that intrinsic motivation was supported when students selected their own books, as compared to having books chosen for them by teachers or other adults. In addition, intrinsic motivation was supported when students acquired strategies for choosing books they could read, for finding interesting books, and for acquiring books for personal ownership. Students who are allowed to choose their own reading materials are more motivated to read, expend more effort, and gain better understanding of the text (Guthrie et al. 2007; Schiefele 1991; Spaulding 1992). Increases in motivation to read have also been reported for a range of students who engaged in self-selected reading, including remedial readers (Mayes 1982) and adolescent students with discipline problems (Coley 1981).

Making Choices About Reading Tasks and Activities. When students have opportunities to select reading tasks and activities that have personal value, they are more likely to engage in higher-order thinking and learning skills (Turner and Paris 1995). In a recent study, students who were allowed to choose their homework assignment from a number of acceptable options reported higher intrinsic motivation, felt more competent, and performed better on unit assessments than students who were assigned homework (Patall, Cooper, and Wynn 2010). The researchers concluded that providing choice is an effective way to support the development of intrinsic motivation.

Turner and Paris (1995) describe classroom literacy experiences in terms of task type. Open tasks were those in which students chose books, learning goals, how they interacted with their peers, and how they completed writing assignments. Closed tasks, on the other hand, were those in which the teacher

For examples of open tasks

see Section 3

determined the reading materials, tasks, and outcomes and students worked individually. Turner and Paris (1995) reported that open literacy tasks were more often associated with intrinsic motivation and persistence than closed literacy tasks.

Teachers can provide choices in a number of ways that will enhance motivation to read. Perks' (2010) 4WH framework is useful for providing students with choices related to reading tasks and activities. **Wh**om will students work with? When reading activities require students to work in groups, as with readers' theater or partner reading, give them some choice about whom they get to work with. **Wh**at strategies/skills will students work with? When tasks and activities are designed to provide opportunities for students to practice specific strategies or skills, the teacher can provide a list of options for students to select from. For example, if the learning objective is to have students demonstrate the sequence of events in a story, the teacher might let students select one activity from the following options: (1) Draw a cartoon to show the sequence of important events in the story, or (2) write a summary paragraph that describes the sequence of the most important events in the story. **Wh**en will students engage in specific reading tasks and activities? Many reading tasks and activities do not have to be completed in a linear fashion. For example, if students are reading text sets of a fiction book and a nonfiction book on the same topic, let the students select the order for reading the texts. **Wh**ere will students read? We are beginning to recognize that students do not always need to sit and work at their desks all day. Let students make simple choices such as whether to stand and read or sit at their desk and read. On sunny days, take them outside, and let them choose where they want to read. In the classroom, when given a choice of where to read, students will find their own "most comfortable" spot. Well-crafted options that provide students with opportunities to make choices about their reading tasks and activities can have a powerful impact on their motivation to read homework (Patall, Cooper, and Wynn 2010).

The *Big* Goal: Supporting Students in Developing Intrinsic Motivation to Read

One thing that we can all agree on is that we would like for our students to find reading personally rewarding. We want our students to be intrinsically motivated to read—we want them to read when no one is looking, when no one is offering candy or pizza. We want them to want to read because we know that literacy is one of, if not *the* cornerstone of academic success and good citizenship. In our view, the central and most important goal of reading instruction is to foster the love of reading. Knowing how to read is not sufficient. Students must have both the skill *and* the will to read. Most important, unless our students are intrinsically motivated to read and choose to engage in reading, they will never reach their full literacy potential.

Moving from Understanding to Practice

In Section 1 we sketched out some of the issues and dilemmas teachers face in trying to figure out how to develop students' intrinsic motivation to read. In this section, we connected some of those issues to research that grounds our understanding of the nature and importance of intrinsic motivation. Now on to Section 3 and the ARC strategies and techniques we have collected from outstanding teachers who do an amazing job of motivating their students to read for joy, not junk!

SECTION 3
BUT THAT

Using the ARC of Motivation to Engage All Readers

BARBARA A. MARINAK and LINDA B. GAMBRELL

Research over the past two decades is clear—teachers matter (Pressley 1997, 1989). The classroom community that teachers create exerts enormous influence on whether or not children will be motivated readers. Deborah Stipek and her colleagues (2002) argue that teachers can motivate students only if they themselves are motivated. Csikszentmihalyi (1991) noted that many teachers know that the best way to engage students in reading activities is to enlist students' interest. They can do this, he suggested, by (a) being sensitive to their goals and desires, (b) offering reading choices, and (c) providing clear and helpful feedback. Guthrie (2011) agrees. He suggests that teachers can deliver instruction that nurtures intrinsic reading motivation by helping students value reading, providing opportunities to engage in relevant literacy experiences, and connecting reading to real-world learning.

In the previous section we shared the research that reveals that rewarding students with junk is not an effective strategy for increasing motivation. Current research suggests that classroom contexts based on principles of motivation that include attention to access, relevance, and choice support the development of intrinsic motivation to read. In other words, as Figure 3–1 illustrates, consider ways to make reading rewarding.

Figure 3–1   Make Reading Rewarding

Avoid tangible, extrinsic rewards such as tokens or food.

- Engage in book blessing.
- Encourage social interaction around books.
- Allows students choice of where and what to read.
- Honor all print.
- Promote reading for a variety of purposes.
- Encourage honest critiques.
- Show examples of a book you didn't like—and explain why.
- Celebrate all reading—not just completion of books.

In this section we take a look at classroom practices that nurture and sustain the development of motivation to read. We focus on classroom practices that reflect the elements of the ARC of motivation: *access*, *relevance*, and *choice*.

The *A* of ARC: Afford *Access* to a Wide Variety of Print

The following suggestions are designed to increase access to print in school as well as invite and celebrate the wide reading students are doing outside of the classroom. Suggestions to increase students' access to print include honoring all print and promoting reading for a variety of purposes. It is challenging to nurture intrinsic motivation when reading takes place only in small groups where text is carefully controlled, especially for reluctant and/or struggling students. When a wide variety of print is read for a variety of reasons, every child in the classroom has multiple opportunities to engage with it. For example, in classrooms where students regularly enjoy reading web articles, jokes and riddles, magazine articles, and sports box scores, everyone, regardless of reading proficiency, can discuss what they read and learned.

Hard as it may seem to believe, not everyone loves everything they read! However, when teachers are passionate about print in their classrooms, children sometimes adopt the notion they too should love everything they read. By making a wide variety of print available, we honor what students love, but we don't necessarily have to love it all ourselves. One example from Barb's classroom days involves reading the much-dreaded snake books. In every elementary classroom Barb ever worked in there was, without a doubt, a group of readers who loved snakes and books about snakes. Barb is an unabashed animal lover—with the exception of snakes. Hence, the perfect opportunity to share one of her reading discomforts. Talking openly about her reluctance to read snake books invited lively debates (and book sharing) whereby the snake lovers tried to sell her on the merits of books such as *Snakes* by Seymour Simon or the Smithsonian's *Everything You Need to Know About Snakes*. And motivation really soared if she brought in an article, website, or book about snakes, explaining that she would *never* read this, but she just knew they would love it! Sometimes their passion was so contagious that Barb actually read some of their favorites (with her eyes averted from the photographs of course!).

Be sure that you, as the teacher, model reading all types of print. Read aloud from an interesting newspaper article, a web fact, a cool list of the most dangerous sea creatures, or a paragraph from the extended glossary of a fascinating informational book. Tell your students about what you read outside of the classroom. Ask them what they read last night. Encourage them to share and make it public. Let it be known that all reading matters!

Recognize Your Super Power!

As we have suggested throughout this book, teachers matter! We are critical to nurturing and supporting the reading motivation of your students, regardless of their age or grade level. Even though they might not look like they care about your feedback and encouragement (as is often the case during adolescence), your words and actions do not go unnoticed. You are a hero, and your super power is the ability to motivate!

More so than dressing in a duck suit or kissing a pig, a steady diet of thoughtful questions and actions can go a long way toward helping your students recognize the relevance of reading. For example, rather than asking, "What are you reading right now?" put passion into that inquiry asking, "What do you *love* reading right now?" (Condon 2014).

Never give up on less engaged or struggling readers. These are the students who need you the most. Set aside time every day to check in with them. Focus on what they read or can read versus what they shy away from or struggle to get through.

Introduce your students to the phrase "avid reader" (Condon 2014). An avid reader is eager or enthusiastic, reading as much and whenever he or she can. Sometimes we are so worried about our less enthusiastic students that we overlook the opportunity to model passion and point out avid reading. Explain to your students how you are an avid reader. Look for avid readers and celebrate their efforts. Involve your students by asking them what such a reader looks and sounds like. Post your definitions of avid reading for all to see—and revise it as necessary. It should be dynamic and ever changing. And last, keep a camera handy. Take photos of avid reading, and post them in your classroom with the header, "Avid Reader . . . That's You!"

Remember to always use your super power for good: Just as you provide students access to a variety of texts, they need access to models of what avid reading looks like. And as you plan ways to increase access to print, recall the words of Voltaire (or Spiderman)—"with great power comes great responsibility." Together, you and your students can create a literacy community where everyone is an avid reader!

Book Blessing

One of the key factors in motivating students to read is a teacher who values reading and is enthusiastic about sharing a love of reading with students. We believe that every teacher can inspire and motivate children to find a lifetime of pleasure and information in the reading of great texts. Linda's many years of research and experiences working in elementary classrooms point to the important role of the teacher. She conducted interviews with children about their reading and found that students spontaneously and consistently made comments about teachers being a motivating influence (Gambrell 1996).

Regardless of grade level, when teachers endorse reading, children listen. When you make a book special—even by something as simple as placing it upright on a table—children are more likely to choose that book over others. Knowing this, we strongly recommend a weekly "blessing of the books" (Gambrell 1996).

To prepare for a book blessing, select ten to twelve books and other print materials you think your children would enjoy reading. Remember that blessing can and should involve all print—bless articles (magazine, newspaper, and web) as well as poems and books of lists. To bless the texts, provide a quick introduction and brief comment about each. After introducing the titles, place them back in the basket so that children can select the ones they want to read. We guarantee they will be in the hands of your students in no time. In fact, your "blessed" collection might become so popular that you need a waiting list! We hope you enjoy a few our favorite book blessings in Figure 3–2.

Figure 3–2 Linda and Barb's Favorite Book Blessings

Linda's Favorites	Barb's Favorites
Pigsty by Mark Teague (fiction)	*A Color of His Own* by Leo Lionni (fiction)
101 Animal Babies by Melvin and Gilda Berger (nonfiction)	*Zipping, Zapping, Zooming Bats* by Ann Early (nonfiction)
Wolf by Becky Bloom (fiction)	*Beast Feast* by Douglas Florian (poetry)
The 10 Deadliest Sea Creatures by Jack Booth (nonfiction)	*Rosie: A Visiting Dog's Story* by Stephanie Calmenson (nonfiction)
Ruby the Copy Cat by Peggy Rathmann (fiction)	*Wild Babies* by Seymour Simon (nonfiction)
What If You Had Animal Teeth!? by Sandra Markle (nonfiction)	*Desert Babies* by Kathy Darling and Tara Darling (nonfiction)
Something from Nothing by Phoebe Gilman (fiction)	*Living Color* by Steve Jenkins (nonfiction)

(continues)

Figure 3–2   *(continued)*

The Camping Trip That Changed America: Theodore Roosevelt, John Muir, and Our National Parks by Barb Rosenstock (nonfiction)	*Keep the Lights Burning, Abbie* by Peter Roop and Connie Roop (nonfiction)
Dumpy La Rue by Elizabeth Winthrop (fiction)	*Eat Your Poison, Dear* by James Howe (fiction)
Do All Spiders Spin Webs? Questions and Answers About Spiders by Melvin and Gilda Berger (nonfiction)	*The Book of North American Owls* by Helen Sattler (nonfiction)

Personal Invitation to Read

Clearly there are times when text must be assigned and read. However, when attempting to increase access to books and nurture motivation for independent reading, try a personal invitation (Marinak, Gambrell, and Mazzoni 2012). Select a text with a specific student in mind, and then personally invite him or her into the reading. Such an invitation can be extended verbally in a one-on-one reading conference or in writing with a special note. Though conversations are important, notes have staying power. Students have told us that they have kept and cherished personal invitations for years—carefully preserving them in a scrapbook or journal. Reading the note became as important as enjoying the selected text.

For the research on why personal interest matters in reading

see Section 2, page 30

A point of clarification regarding extending personal invitations: You must be willing to think way outside the box. This can be especially true when attempting to nurture intrinsic motivation in reluctant and/or struggling readers. Sometimes it's all about presentation. Barb admits to devising some wild and crazy personal invitations to read. She has wrapped books in paper illustrated with the child's favorite animal, used the sports page to entice a reluctant reader into an article about his preferred team, and decorated plain white paper with galaxy stickers to convince a struggling reader that she would love *Comets, Stars, the Moon, and Mars: Space Poems and Paintings* by Douglas Florian.

By far, one of the most interesting invitations Barb has created was for a reluctant sixth grader. She knew this student might enjoy mysteries. This was a tough one because Barb suspected the student would never want to be seen accepting a book or openly carrying a book— she showed great disdain for any peers who expressed joy in reading. The brown paper bag in which the students carried lunch to school each day was an inspiration. Barb wrapped *Assassin*, the first of a mystery series, in a brown paper bag and quietly passed it to the student in the hall. The student accepted the bag without a word. The next day, the student slipped Barb a note that said, "I LOVED it. Do you have more? And if you ever tell anyone I am reading, I won't take any more." A whole series of books traveled quietly, clothed in brown paper bags.

Matching an invitation to a reader is not difficult and need not be costly. With knowledge of the child and a little imagination, teachers can help students discover their new favorite "read." Used wrapping paper, newspaper, and greeting cards can be recycled. Stickers, decorative bags, and colorfully printed invitations are inexpensive at end-of-the season sidewalk sales. Figure 3–3 shows one teacher's note that accompanied a book wrapped in the comics pages from the newspaper.

Figure 3–3 Mrs. Manley's Personal Invitation to Read

Dear James,

This is a personal invitation to read the new Batman comic book. I wrapped it in comics from the Sunday paper. Hope you love both the comic book and my gift wrapping.

Mrs. Manley

There is nothing more affirming than knowing an important person in a child's life (their teacher) has selected a book, poem, or article just for him or her. Inherent in a personal invitation to read is honoring a student's interests as well as the message that you can't wait to hear whether he or she enjoyed your pick. In other words, in addition to inviting reading, you are welcoming the conversation.

Picture This!

Many state standards remind us that literacy is defined as reading, writing, listening, speaking, viewing, and representing. Recognizing that many things can be read (books, magazines, newspapers, signs, menus, etc.), the same is true for representing. There are many ways to represent reading experiences. One interesting idea, the visual interview, is borrowed from the art world. A visual interview is answering questions with illustrations or photos rather than words. These questions could be posed by the teacher or created in small groups by students. Visual interviews can be used to increase access to print by inviting children to pictorially represent what they have read or what they would like to read. Children can respond to visual interview questions written by the teacher or a peer. Image responses can be illustrated, pictures taken by the child, or non-copyrighted images borrowed from the web such as book jackets or

> **Providing choice in how students respond to their reading is important**
>
> see Section 2, page 30

free photographs. Visual interviews provide practice writing questions and tap into the creative, representational skills necessary to convey an answer using only images. Figure 3–4 provides a form for the visual interview.

Figure 3–4 Sarah's Visual Interview

1. What was your favorite book in kindergarten?	Sarah's drawing or photo goes here.
2. Who is your favorite author now?	Sarah's drawing or photo goes here.
3. What would you like to read about next?	Sarah's drawing or photo goes here.

Visual interviews could be themed or not. A themed interview might ask for pictorial representations of favorite seasonal readings or topics of interesting magazine articles. And one that all children are sure to love is a visual interview that asks them to illustrate or take photos of their favorite places to read. And yes, it's OK to draw or take a photo of the bathroom—as long as it's not in use!

Conducting and sharing visual interviews can introduce children to titles, genres, authors, or subjects they may not have been familiar with or thought about as a print topic. Access to and conversations about reading can be stimulated through interesting questions paired with fascinating images.

Selecting Books for the Library

In interviews conducted during several of our studies, one of the comments we heard repeatedly when discussing school and classroom libraries was, "Why do teachers always get to pick the books?" Students wondered why they don't have some voice in selecting the texts for their libraries, and they openly expressed a desire to be part of the process. For example, in a study we conducted, students were asked to read from several books and help us make book selections for the school library (Marinak and Gambrell 2008). During their school day, they were given the opportunity to choose an activity to engage in during "free time" (jigsaw puzzles, math games, reading). We expected that the students would mention what they chose to participate in during this time. To our surprise all of the third-grade students who participated in the study reported that helping to select books for their library was the "most fun" activity. Inherent in the questions and responses from our studies is the desire and willingness of children to take ownership of their reading materials.

You can invite children to select books for the school or classroom library in a variety of ways. Reading interest surveys can be conducted with the class. If surveys are used, remember to tell students how their survey responses will be used in text selection. As these "recommended" books are added to the classroom library, be sure to profile the books or magazines and acknowledge the student or students who made the recommendation. For example, "Thanks to Mark Brown and Mike Jones for requesting the new Matt Christopher book. Here it is. Enjoy!"

Other ways to allow students to participate in text selection is to ask for book committee volunteers. Teachers and the librarian can then meet with grade-level or cross-grade-level committees. The committees can discuss topics and titles. Browsing library book/periodical websites and catalogs can help promote discussion.

And finally, when new books or periodicals come into the library, book committee members can spread the word. Invite committee members to be the first to browse new purchases. Allow them to brainstorm ways they can "sell" the new purchases to their friends. In addition to growing ownership in school and classroom libraries, inviting children into the selection process nurtures reading motivation by fostering a personal relationship between the keepers (teachers and librarians) and users. Interestingly, this notion of a personal relationship with libraries is not a new idea. Samuel S. Green of the Worcester Free Public Library wrote about it in 1876. His sentiments are worth pondering today as we work to increase access to print for all students:

> **Access to print includes opportunities to read a wide variety of text as well as engage with other avid readers.**

If you gain the respect and confidence of readers, and they find you easy to get at and pleasant to talk with, great opportunities are afforded of stimulating the love of study and of directing investigators to the best sources of information.

You find out what books the actual users of the library need, and our judgment improves in regard to the kind of books it is best to add to it. You see what subjects the constituency of the institution are interested in.

One of the best means of making a library popular is to mingle freely with its users, and help them in every way. When this policy is pursued for a series of years in any town, a very large portion of the citizens receive answers to questions, and the conviction spreads through the community that the library is an institution of such beneficent influences that it cannot be dispensed with. (Green 1876, 1)

Wonderful words from a very wise man. Libraries, a fascinating and heavily used collection of reading materials are, as Green noted, indispensible. Increasing access to and interest in such collections means inviting children into every facet of what makes libraries wonderful. Clearly the print is important, but as Green also reminds us, so too are the relationships formed between readers, teachers, and librarians. "In conclusion, I wish to say that there are few pleasures comparable to that of associating continually with curious and vigorous young minds, and of aiding them in realizing their ideals" (Green 1876, 2).

Engaging Students in Fact Checking

As anyone who works with children knows, opinions and ideas abound. Rarely does the question, "Who knows about _____ (fill in the blank)?" go unanswered. Children know (or think they know) a lot. Of course the problem is that sometimes their knowledge is incomplete or inaccurate. A variation of an anticipation guide (Head and Readence 1986) can be a motivating and strategic way to grow or revise students' knowledge by accessing texts for verification. Strictly speaking, an anticipation guide is used to consider predictions, anticipate text, and verify the predictions. By agreeing or disagreeing with a series of statements before reading, students connect new information to prior knowledge, thereby growing self-concept and heightening the motivation to read.

A variation of an anticipation guide can be compared to the political fact checking often done by journalists. In other words, just because one says it's so does not necessarily mean it is so. Fact checking can certainly be done before reading. However, the process is even more powerful after reading complex texts when comprehension confusions are more likely to occur. Fact checking supports numerous Common Core State Standards (2012) such as formulating assertions, gathering relevant information from multiple print and digital sources, assessing the credibility and accuracy of each source, and using text to support an answer or build a

> This kind of activity empowers readers to read widely, develop assertions, and search for verification.

case. As you can see from Matthew's search in Figure 3–5, fact checking can help students revise their assertions as well as lead to new and interesting questions . . . and more research! And to raise the rigor even more, teachers might require two sources for fact verification.

Figure 3–5 Fact-Check Yourself

Yes, it is true	No, it is not true	Not sure Maybe It depends

Matthew's initial assertion: Cheetahs are the fastest animal.

Assertion/Revision/ Question	Result	Source/Answer
Cheetahs are the fastest animal.		www.extremescience.com/cheetah.htm It depends. Cheetahs are the fastest creatures in the world *on land*. They can run 70 miles per hour.

Clarifying his initial assertion led to more interesting questions and research.

Assertion/ Revision/ Question	Result	Source/Answer
Cheetahs are the fastest animal.		www.extremescience.com/cheetah.htm It depends. Cheetahs are the fastest creatures in the world *on land*. They can run 70 miles per hour.
The blue whale is the fastest creature in water.		www.livescience.com/32772-what -animal-is-the-fastest-swimmer.html No, it is the sailfish. They have been clocked at 68 miles per hour.
What is the fastest flying animal?		http://earthsky.org/earth/fastest-bird It depends. The peregrine falcon can dive up to 200 miles an hour. However, the great snipe can fly 4,200 miles at 60 miles per hour.

The use of fact checking, as informed by anticipation guides (Head and Readence 1986), increases access to text by releasing responsibility for assertion verification back to students. It is only by reading, rereading, and researching a wide variety of credible sources that readers can be confident in their knowledge.

The *R* of ARC: Invite Children into *Relevant* Reading Experiences

Formally and informally, in ways that are more and less overt, students seek relevance in learning. We have all heard and seen evidence of the important of relevance in the classroom. Inquisitive (and sometimes frustrated) children will ask, "Why do I need to learn this?" More reticent students will fade quietly into the background, not being a disruption but clearly not learning. Sometimes the question "Why are we doing this?" is a challenge for teachers to answer. Making the case for literacy in all aspects of life is not hard. The trick is to invite real-life reading and writing experiences into our everyday instruction. Though sometimes not easy in an age of high-stakes assessment, nurturing intrinsic reading motivation must include engaging children in relevant reading experiences.

We can motivate students to read by establishing relevance in our reading instruction. The examples that follow are designed to involve students in decision making, promote self-directed learning, and create opportunities for self-expression—all key ingredients in nurturing intrinsic reading motivation. Because, as Brophy notes, there should be "good reasons for developing lessons, and we should articulate these good reasons to students during instruction" (2004, 141).

Promote Personal Enjoyment of Reading

Barb's early days as a literacy coach marked the beginning of the schoolwide reading incentive craze. BOOK IT! was looming large. School administrators were getting their heads shaved (males), sitting in dunk tanks, or having pies thrown at them, all in effort to entice kids to read. Her building was no different. Everyone thought it was vital to implement a schoolwide reading incentive program. However, the principal was not getting his head shaved (nor was Barb), and no one was getting dunked or splattered with food. You will recall from Chapter 1 that we arranged an incentive program whereby kids read their way to a movie night. We called it "Duck Away with a Book." Cute title and our intentions were honorable. We so wanted our students to value reading that Barb flapped and quacked her way through the halls on kickoff day. Though great fun (for the students and Barb), dressing up as a duck was not relevant to reading.

I must admit to still participating in attention-grabbing stunts! The difference now is that we plan for ways to sustain initial enthusiasm by thinking about relevancy. One of those actions is to constantly, overtly, and passionately promote the personal enjoyment of reading.

> **Knowing your students well is key to getting them hooked on reading as noted in Section 2.**

One idea that has worked for us in a range of settings with virtually all ages is to link personal interests with print. Sounds simple right? Not always. Some children are shy and quiet or don't choose to openly share what they enjoy. Learning what makes kids tick might necessitate prowling the places where casual conversations happen—the cafeteria, the playground, and around lockers. To illustrate the importance of these less formal spaces, I recall a particularly poignant moment shared by Carolyn, an early childhood colleague. While out on the playground one day, she noticed Anna picking up rocks. Without malice (or knowledge), Carolyn directed Anna to put them down. It was not until a few weeks later that my colleague realized her mistake. Carolyn was looking through pictures taken by Anna for another project and in the collection was a photo of a bookshelf on Anna's front porch. The three shelves contained a wide variety of carefully displayed stones. When asked about the picture, Anna proudly replied that it was her "rockatopia"—her beloved rock collection. In that moment Carolyn realized what Anna was doing on the playground. Promoting the pleasure of reading for this little girl meant linking her interests (rocks) with text (so many options!). She loved the books and articles provided by her now-knowledgeable teacher! Other links we have made include connecting kids who play Angry Birds (the video game) to the real *Angry Birds* (White 2012)—a wildly creative series of books by National Geographic. Another one is introducing movie fans of Indiana Jones to the character's book series. You get the idea . . . whatever it takes to learn about children and pair their passions with print!

And finally, consider ways to make print prominent in your classroom and school. Invite VIPs (the school librarian and principal) into your classroom regularly to "sell" books or announce a subscription to a cool new magazine. And why not feature print as part of the morning announcements? We proclaim many other important messages; let's make reading one of them. And by this we don't mean announcing the names of accomplished readers—we mean profiling print. Feature quick book reviews or announcements of new materials that have arrived.

Promoting personal enjoyment underscores that reading is relevant. Be deliberate about sending the message that it happens everywhere, all day long, and for a wide variety of purposes.

Celebrate Students' Reading Lives

There is nothing more relevant, and motivating, than to honor the significant books in a child's life. Your Reading Life (Marinak, Gambrell, and Mazzoni 2012) invites them to do so! This wonderful celebration embodies relevance in several important ways: (a) recognizing and remembering the listening and reading taking place at home, (b) solidifying the connection between the important people in a child's life and print, (c) encouraging conversations at home about all kinds of print, and (d) providing teachers with important insights about the literacy lives of their students outside of school. And once again, as you invite children to share their reading life, remind them that you are anxious to hear about all the important print they have shared with family and friends. Figure 3–6 contains brief directions for getting started with Your Reading Life. Figure 3–7 is an example of fifth-grade teacher Jeff Hampton's model. And Figure 3–8 is third grader Joseph's reading life.

Your Reading Life invites children and their families to revisit the print they have shared. It celebrates that reading is and always has been a huge part of their lives. Thinking and talking about past readings, connecting them to important people and events, and being invited to share their experiences reminds children that they have and always will read for purpose and pleasure!

Figure 3–6 Your Reading Life: Getting Started

1. Explain to children that they will have the opportunity to share their reading life.

2. Model examples from your reading life. Show children several of the important reading experiences from your life. Discuss what else was happening in your life and how each book connected to important events.

3. Explain to children that going home and talking to family is the first step in making their My Reading Life timeline. Reminiscing with family and revisiting the family library will help them remember favorite read-alouds and books.

4. After talking with family, children can begin their timeline. In addition to compiling a list, invite children to connect the book with life by writing down what was happening at the time they heard or read each title.

5. Provide a time for children to share their reading life!

Figure 3–7 Mr. Hampton's Reading Life

Title	What Was Happening in My Life?	How Old Was I?	Did I Find a Copy to Share?
One Fish, Two Fish, Red Fish, Blue Fish (Dr. Seuss)	After reading this book, I asked my parents for a fish tank. I got one and started collecting very colorful fish.	5	Yes, I still have my original copy.
Woodsong (Gary Paulsen)	I read this book about Gary Paulsen training and racing sled dogs when I was in fifth grade. Late, as an adult, I visited Alaska to see the finish of Iditarod.	11	Yes, and our library has a copy signed by Mr. Paulsen.

Title	What Was Happening in My Life?	How Old Was I?	Did I Find a Copy to Share?
Eye to Eye: How Animals See the World (Steve Jenkins)	This is a brand-new book. I have been reading it over the past few days in preparation for our animal survival unit next week.	Right now!	For sure, it is the "featured book" in our classroom library.

Figure 3–8 Joseph's Reading Life

Title	What Was Happening in My Life?	How Old Was I?	Did I Find a Copy to Share?
The Lorax (Dr. Seuss)	My grandma read this book to me over the phone. She lives in California where people are trying to save the giant redwood trees.	5	No, but I think our library has a copy.
Big Book of Dinosaurs (DK Publishing)	I *loved* this book when I was in first grade. I actually still like it. After reading this book, my parents took me to the Chicago Field Museum, and I saw Sue, the T. rex. Awesome!	6	Yes, I have a copy and can bring it in.

(continues)

Figure 3–8 *(continued)*

Title	What Was Happening in My Life?	How Old Was I?	Did I Find a Copy to Share?
Curiosity Rover Report at http://www.nasa.gov	I want to be an astronaut when I grow up so I read the NASA website all the time. Did you know Curiosity tweets?	Right now— I am 9.	Sure, anyone can go to nasa.gov and read about the Mars rovers.

> **Social media is a great way to create a community of readers.**

Book Tweets

Let's face it, Twitter is cool! Tweets are short, 140-character messages that provide another means of promoting the relevance of reading.

What a great way to encourage reading chats and increase access to a wide variety of text and opinions! Book tweets are messages written by readers (your students, you, the librarian, principal, etc.) and posted on a Twitter board (classroom bulletin board or whiteboard). However, before book tweeting, children need to know and follow the rules of Twitter. Figure 3–9 contains a few rules for book tweets. Figure 3–10 is an example of two book tweets grouped by hash tags.

Book tweets are a motivating way to encourage everyone in your literacy community to share their reading thoughts. Make sure you model a few messages, and ask other teachers as well as the librarian and principal to tweet or reply. In addition to inviting an interactive, ongoing conversation about print, book tweets also provide practice summarizing and selecting words carefully. Like poems, great tweets are constructed only after pondering each and every word. Thinking about words and careful writing are relevant skills that transcend book tweets!

Figure 3–9 Rules of Book Tweets

- Tweet must be about a book, poem, or article you have recently read.
- The tweet can be no more than 140 characters.
- Remember that characters include spaces and punctuation marks.
- Begin your book tweet with a hashtag.
- A hashtag is a word or an unspaced phrase that begins with the hash character (#).
- Remember that your hashtag should include your first name and words that summarize the text.
- Hashtags will let us group your tweet with similar book tweets.
- Include a reply box in your book tweet.

Figure 3–10 Examples of Book Tweets Categorized by Hashtags

#BrianLovesWolves	#EmilyHearsHowling
I loved *Wolves* by Seymour Simon. Very cool pictures! My favorite is the wolves running in the snow.	I read about wolves on the National Geographic website. Howling is how packs talk to each other.
Reply	Reply

Form Book Clubs

A group of fifth graders reminded us of the role socialization and discussion plays in nurturing intrinsic reading motivation. While working in an elementary school where the principal and teachers were concerned about the low motivation of their fifth graders, we decided to "listen in" to their conversations during a typical day. In an effort to grow interest, these teachers were providing self-selected reading

(SSR) time every day, just as numerous studies have suggested. But, as consumers of research, we need to remember that results are not always generalizable from one situation to another. And gosh, were we quickly reminded of this! When the teachers announced it was time for SSR, several students in unison proclaimed, "Great! Time to sit down, shut up, and read!" Our students were sending us a not-so-subtle message: They wanted something different, and the only way to find out the reason for their displeasure and address it was to talk with them. We learned that it was not the reading they disliked—it was the lack of opportunity to talk about what they were reading. One student proposed a solution: "Why can't we have a book club?"

Through the reading of several studies about book clubs (Gavelek and Raphael 1996; Raphael, Florio-Ruane, and George 2001) we established the parameters for our book clubs. And do notice, we established multiple clubs in order to encourage students to participate in a wide range of text choices and discussions. Figure 3–11 summarizes our guidelines. It is also important to note that this team morphed SSR to include book clubs. Independent reading was not eliminated; we tried to strike a balance. The fifth-grade teachers believed, and we agreed, that the opportunity to sit quietly and read a book of choice for a sustained period of time was very important. Hence, this building's six-day instructional cycle became three days of independent reading and three days of book clubs.

As Raphael, Florio-Ruane, and George (2001) suggest, when students interact with each other, their thinking becomes public, and they have the opportunity to hear the language of literacy. During these conversations, readers can use language to achieve their collective and personal goals. The emphatic request by our fifth graders was a relevant reminder that they wanted to engage with books in a real-world way. After all, as we said to each other during book club planning, what is the first thing you want to do when you read something interesting? Talk about it, of course!

Research suggests that collaboration nurtures engaged reading.

Figure 3–11 Parameters for Book Clubs

1. Be sure to balance book clubs with SSR or DEAR (drop everything and read) time.

2. Create four to six book clubs that include a wide array of reading options—fiction, nonfiction, poetry, newspaper, magazines, websites, and so on. One of our most popular book clubs was centered on current events in which students tracked "big stories" (approved by the teacher) across a variety of sources—fabulous practice identifying perspectives.

3. Rotate the book clubs frequently to afford many opportunities to read a wide variety of texts. In upper elementary classes, we were able to rotate about every two or three weeks.

4. Allow each club to decide on the amount of reading to be completed before the next meeting. We were thrilled with the expectations student set for themselves.

5. Establish a rule that students must read prior to coming to book club. Our students discovered very quickly that if they had not completed their agreed-upon reading, it was impossible to meaningfully participate in the discussion. Some tried but to no avail.

6. We suggest teachers select the text for the first several book club rotations. If all goes well, students can certainly be invited to offer suggestions.

7. After the text for each rotation has been established and discussed, have students vote, on paper, which club they would like to join. No need for chaos when eliciting book club wishes. In addition, teachers need the discretion to form clubs after considering student choices as many other variables (behavior, learning needs, and so on). We asked our students to give up their first two choices, promising that we would do our best to give them one of the two options. In tracking their requests over several marking periods, we found we were able to honor one of their two choices over 95 percent of the time.

Listen Actively

Yes, an important and often overlooked way to nurture relevance and intrinsic motivation is to actively listen as children discuss their reading. Sounds simple . . . right? Not always. In an age of sometimes crushing curricular expectations and high-stakes testing, teachers feel pressured to teach as much as possible. And, let's face it—it takes time to listen, and time is precious in today's classrooms. But three decades of research related to listening and academic achievement and, specifically, the impact of listening on reading proficiency and motivation should convince us that taking the time is worth it (Christensen and James 2008, Clark and Moss 2011; Hidi and Harackiewicz 2000; Lapp et al. 2013).

In order to help all students see the relevance of reading, research indicates that teachers must listen for and encourage individual interests, strategies, and reasoning abilities. We should listen to children as they read and discuss the text in order to fully understand their spontaneous comments and responses (Clark and Moss 2011; Hohmann, Weikart, and Epstein 1995; Lapp et al. 2013).

As you plan literacy instruction, consider ways you can set aside time to actively listen. Reading and writing conferencing is an authentic and relevant way to do this. And remember that listening is not the same as hearing. Hearing refers to the sounds gathered by your auditory system. Listening requires much more. Focus and commitment to the speaker are needed in order to actively listen. This means paying attention not only to the conversation but how the message is being conveyed. As the active listener, you must attend to the use of language and voice as well as the important nonverbal cues such as proximity, eye contact, intonation, infection, and gesture.

It has been helpful to us to keep the following suggestions in mind as we actively listen to readers (Marinak, Strickland, and Keat 2010):

- **Stop Talking**

    Once again, this sounds simple, but often is not. Children, especially very young students and English learners, need time to gather and finish their thoughts. Essentially, it is a reminder to take the "wait time" as students ponder our questions. When a student is talking, do not interrupt, talk over them, or finish his or her sentences.

- **Support the Comfort of Your Speaker**

    Nonverbal behaviors are powerful. They can encourage a speaker to continue or close down a conversation. To support the comfort of speakers, consider their needs and concerns. Nod, use gestures, and maintain eye contact to encourage and reassure them you are listening.

- **Be Patient**

    A pause, even a long pause, does not necessarily mean the child is finished. Be patient and let them continue at his or her own pace.

- **Silence Is Golden**

    Let there be some silence to give the child thinking time. Don't feel that you need to fill the verbal voids.

- **Create a Listening Space in Your Mind**

    Actively create a space in your mind that is empty of your own assumptions, so you can hear each child's way of understanding the world. After a student has finished talking, repeat or rephrase what he or she said in order to ensure that you understood the message.

    > Listening means creating an audience for children. And one of the best ways to pull children forward into literacy is to become an active, interested audience in their reading lives.

    It is only by actively listening that you can learn about the likes, dislikes, comforts, and discomforts related to what your students are saying about what they are reading. Genuine interest, as demonstrated by active listening, is motivating.

Who Knew?

One of the goals of today's literacy standards is providing students with the strategies and dispositions necessary to function in dynamic and unpredictable academic and real-world settings (college and career). We want them to learn to research, think, problem solve, and write like scientists, engineers, historians, mathematicians, musicians, artists, and coaches. In essence, this type of literacy instruction is, at its core, the definition of relevance. For example, historians are constantly looking for the relationships between concepts and documents. When scientists are solving a problem, they seek answers to cause-and-effect relationships. This work is grounded in relevance, the understanding of how one topic is connected to another in a way that makes it useful to consider. Therefore, if we want students to engage in relevant reading and experience real-world dialogue, we must integrate the web into our daily instruction. Try to share at least one fact, blog post, or article from the web every day with the purpose of elaborating on a topic, offering a new perspective, or clarifying a confusion. Think about doing "Who knew _____?" using the article du jour. Figure 3–12 is an example from a classroom we recently visited.

Figure 3–12 Who Knew?

What's on the Web Today?

The Giant Magellan telescope will help astronomers unravel the mysteries of the cosmos.

We'll read about it today at

www.gmto.org/

Using web articles written by experts allows students not only to read breaking stories that have not made their way into print yet but to also gain insight into how professionals grapple with relevance in their field. One recent example of the importance of the web occurred during a classroom discussion about owls. The class was reading *The Book of North American Owls* by Helen Sattler and preparing to dissect owl pellets when Aaron declared, "Dr. M., I know what that sound is called when owls throw up pellets. It's called yarping!" Believing I was fairly well versed in all things owls, I replied to Aaron that I had not heard that term. I asked where he learned it. He explained that he had read it in a book. My missed opportunity in that quick exchange is that I failed to ask Aaron which book. I assumed he had read it in a work of nonfiction. While the students were at recess, I headed for the web where Google and a web glossary saved the day. I quickly learned that Aaron was reading *The Guardians of Ga'Hoole* by Kathryn Lasky, a fantasy series about a band of noble owls. In the world of Ga'Hoole, yarping means "the action of an owl expelling a pellet from its beak, a few hours after its meal; an owl in serious distress may also start yarping" (Wikia 2014, 1).

After recess, we had a fascinating discussion about the language Lasky used to create the Guardian world. Even more amazing was the epistemological scavenger hunt that unfolded. We learned that the word *yarping* was making its way into our everyday language. A quick search revealed an article about senators in Congress "yarping" at each other and that "yarping" had become a call sign of computer hackers.

In this case, the web created a motivating moment. Googling can be fun! However, we recommend being much more deliberate when integrating web content into literacy instruction. Look to web-based resources as a way to share simulations, take a virtual field trip, view live cams, provide primary source documents, or contribute to a blog. Encourage your students to pull the thread between more traditional print and web articles. Show them how professionals communicate with each other in the virtual world. Experience relevance by seeing, in real time, how ideas are connected.

The *C* of ARC: Afford as Much *Choice* as Possible

The need for choice is important for all students, but it is especially crucial for children who find literacy daunting. As Worthy and colleagues (Worthy et al. 2001) contend, there is a critical human factor when attempting to reach struggling readers. They suggest that a "personalized, responsive, relationship-based approach combined with interesting and appropriate text and student choice" (195) may indeed be the only way to begin nurturing the skill and will to read. When planning for these children it is helpful to begin by considering motivation first.

Allowing students to make choices about their reading material will increase the likelihood that they will engage more in reading. However, given instructional expectations and district mandates, it is sometimes difficult to find ways to offer choice. We hope the suggestions that follow are easy, curricular-considerate ways to afford a wide variety of literacy choices.

Promote Library Values

One of the most disturbing trends we have seen in recent years that clearly erode intrinsic reading motivation is restricting access to books and periodicals in the library. There appear to be two reasons for this: (a) the desire on the part of teachers or librarians to guide children to books "on their level," and (b) the leveling of materials is suggested by a schoolwide or classroom incentive program. Accelerated Reader (AR) is the most widely used program that recommends allowing children to read only with the discrete colored levels (e.g., orange, double orange, etc.).

First, we must recall that children do not possess a single reading level. They are able to read print of varying levels, depending upon prior knowledge, interest, support, and tenacity. Hence, an attempt to match text to reader in the library where the core value is choice is an ill-advised action and one that could result in eroding intrinsic motivation. Second, numerous researchers have argued passionately against the parameters suggested by many reading incentive programs. Mallette, Henk, and Melnick (2004) found that AR did not positively influence recreational attitudes toward reading and that it negatively influenced self-perception in low-achieving male readers. Stephen Krashen (2005) writes that there is no evidence that AR increases reading achievement or improves attitudes toward reading. In addition, Schmidt (2008, 210) suggests that the AR teaches children that "reading is more about numbers and efficiency than learning from or enjoying books."

In order to create and sustain the kind of vibrant book exchange envisioned by Benjamin Franklin in 1727, we suggest adopting library values. Make your classroom and school libraries a place where choice is always honored. The American Library Association (ALA) has many resources available to help schools promote library values. A few we believe worthy of serious consideration (ALA 2014) include:

- Access—All information resources provided by the library should be readily, equally, and equitably accessible to all library users.
- Diversity—A nation's diversity should be valued, and we should strive to reflect that diversity in library collections.
- The Public Good—Libraries are an essential public good and are fundamental institutions in democratic societies.

In conclusion, promoting library values means affording your children the same freedom and privileges you expect in a library. Imagine how you would feel if someone tapped you on the shoulder in the library and said, "Sorry, I don't think you will understand that book," or "No, you are not allowed to borrow from that section." Library programs rooted in these core values have a lasting effect on language growth, reading development, and overall achievement (ALA 2104; Niegaard 1994).

> **Promoting reading engagement is ongoing work. We have to be mindful of ways we may unintentionally be disengaging previously engaged readers.**

Offer Choice of Teacher Read-Aloud

As we noted in *Selecting Books for the Library*, several of the studies we have collaborated on (Marinak, Mazzoni, and Gambrell 2012; Marinak and Gambrell 2009) reveal children's desire to be involved in selecting books. These interview studies indicated that children wanted to help pick materials for classroom and school libraries. The other area in which students expressed a desire for choice is the teacher read-aloud. Students often shared the notion that they did not enjoy the teacher read-aloud because "he/she never asks me what I want to hear," "he/she always reads girl books," or "he/she never reads things I am interested in." Inviting students to help select the teacher read-aloud is a powerful and easy way to offer choice (Marinak, Gambrell, and Malloy 2012). In fact, when this is an option in classrooms, we have been amazed by the newfound enthusiasm for the teacher read-aloud.

To engage students in the selection process, we suggest beginning with a book blessing (see page 38). Collect a variety of books, articles, and magazines that would lend themselves to a read-aloud, and spend a few minutes introducing each. These previews should be brief and especially designed to pique interest but not give too much away. After the book blessing, place the materials in a basket, and explain that students will be asked to recommend their first and second choices for the next teacher read-aloud. Invite readers to browse the potential read-alouds for a couple of days before making their selections. When we, and others, have implemented this option, the pre-choice conversations have been astounding. We have heard children say things like "if you put down my first choice this week, I'll go with your first choice next time," or "if we all put this as our first choice, there's more of a chance she will read it." Being so motivated to hear text that they negotiate choices with each other is music to our ears!

After several days of browsing, ask students for their first and second choices. As we suggested with book clubs, choices should be written. Also, we found that by affording choice of the teacher read-aloud on a regular basis, most students hear their first or second selection every few weeks.

Allow Students to Choose the What, Where, and How

The What and Where. One of the most basic and important choices we must afford students involves the sacred time we set aside for independent reading. Allowing readers to select their own materials as well as where they would like to read supports the development of autonomy as it relates to literacy engagement. It takes time and practice for children to become autonomous and self-reliant while reading. Offering choices encourages them to read widely, take risks, and persevere when material they selected becomes challenging, all critical lifelong literacy behaviors (Gambrell 2011; Wigfield and Guthrie 2000).

You should consider several parameters when providing independent reading choice including the *what and where*. We suggest that there be a time each day when children have the freedom to choose *whatever* they want to read *wherever* they want to read it. You might know this opportunity by the terms *independent reading*; *sustained, silent reading* (a term we don't care for because it need not be silent; there should be teacher-student interaction and, in some cases, student-to-student interaction as well)*; self-selected reading*; or *drop everything and read (DEAR) time*. At this time, all print is honored (books, newspapers, magazines, web articles, etc.). And, as much as possible, allow children to select a comfy spot to enjoy their selections (Miller and Moss 2013).

Barb had an experience a few years ago that reinforced the importance of text choice and how cranky kids can become when we restrict it in ways that seem incongruent with the values being promoted. She was working with a school that was concerned about the lack of reading engagement observed in students. In an attempt to promote reading motivation, a thirty-minute independent reading block (IRB) was set aside. Sounds great, right? While talking with the students several weeks after the IRB was implemented, it became clear that mistakes had been made. When Barb asked how they were enjoying the new choice time, the overwhelming reply was "Hate it!" A few more questions got at some of the problems: too many rules during what was to be a time for choice. Students were required to read only fiction, and they had to read at their seats. They were not permitted to go to the computer lab, library, or other areas with comfortable chairs. With no ill intent, the faculty had implemented the program without thinking through effective ways to promote independent reading and nurture intrinsic motivation. The result was that students were more unhappy about reading than before the project was implemented. After hearing the negative feedback from students, IRB was revised. Free choice meant free choice—all print was honored, as were comfy spaces to read. Students were then much more motivated to read!

Allowing students to choose the *what and where* does take careful planning, whether it is in an individual classroom or a schoolwide endeavor. In order to nurture intrinsic motivation during your independent reading time, it's worth having periodic conversations with your students regarding the luxury of being able to read anything they want, wherever they choose.

The How. It is also possible to afford choice during reading instruction. First, teachers often want to hold children accountable in some fashion for independent reading. This practice often entails keeping a log of reading titles. An interesting twist on traditional reading logs is a reading book of lists. We know that children love list books, whether it is a book of world records or the top-ten list of the most dangerous animals. They love books containing lists of sports records, mind-boggling trivia, curious tidbits, animal facts, and so forth. So, why not invite students to engage in creating their own listography? Encourage them to keep track of their independent reads in a book of lists whereby they can record their reads under category headers of their choice. For example, Stewart, in his "My Reading Book of Lists," placed *Dew Drop Dead* by James Howe under the headers "Loved It," "A Great Mystery," "Cool Cover," and "I Wore It Out." Imagine what you could learn by browsing your children's reading lists! *Dew Drop Dead* (Howe 2000) is clearly a keeper for Stewart. Wonder how many times he read it to earn a spot under "Wore It Out"? Figure 3–13 is a short, and by no means exhaustive, list of headers for a reading book of lists. Challenge your children to be creative in their choice of headers, and remind them that their reads can appear on multiple lists.

Figure 3–13   Listography

- Loved It
- Loved the Cover
- Loved the Illustrations
- Loved the Photographs
- I Learned So Much
- Wore These Out
- Recommended These to a Friend
- Want to Read Another by This Author
- Teacher Read-Alouds I Enjoyed
- Favorite . . .
- Not My Favorite
- Books I Might Skip
- Characters I Would Like to Spend Time With
- Want to Read It

The final suggestion for choosing *the how* of reading involves allowing your students to decide how they might respond to texts. Responding to reading is clearly an important aspect of growing proficiency; however, it can and should include nontraditional options. One of our studies revealed that students often tire of writing chapter summaries and completing workbook pages (Marinak and Gambrell 2009). When possible, allow students to choose their reading response. This can be done individually or through interesting negotiation in small groups.

Yet another way to offer response choice in a larger or longer reading unit is to allow children to construct their own contract options for responding. Invite them to brainstorm options for responding to each piece of text being read during the unit. Barb has used student-created contracts in virtually all grade levels and for all types of text. In addition to watching motivation grow as children personalize their responses, she never ceases to be amazed at the rigor they take on without any external expectations. It was during one of these contract opportunities that Barb learned the critical lesson that "no response" *is* a response. In other words, there are times when children should be granted the space to not respond. This is especially true when reading involves difficult or disturbing material. This lesson came during a Holocaust unit in grade six. The reading involved several pieces of historical fiction and a number of informational books. On one particular day, when asked to complete their contract, the response was . . . silence. Barb and her colleague realized they were at a point in the unit where the gravity of the subject matter was beginning to resonate. Clearly, their students needed the freedom to not respond and time to just sit, ponder, and talk in whispers. From that day on, many of their contracts were built with "silence" as a reading response.

Allowing students to choose the what, where, and how includes many options for recognizing and nurturing autonomy. The suggestions above are appropriate for virtually all ages and grade levels and can be easily adapted to most independent or instructional situations.

Let It Rain! And Other Enticing Book Displays

We can invite children into a wide variety of print by taking a hint from libraries and booksellers: Creative displays get attention. Consider how often you have been motivated to read a book after browsing an attractive display. Traditional bookshelves with only spines displayed are not very eye-catching, especially for struggling or reluctant readers.

So, to increase access to your classroom library, "let it rain" by employing nontraditional book displays (Trelease 2015). For example, plastic or light metal rain gutters can be easily affixed to bulletin boards, transforming them into front-cover rows of browsing pleasure. Rain-gutter shelves use the power of book jacket art to introduce children to the book. If rain gutters can't be erected due to space limitations, large pocket charts or shoe trees that fit over a door are other options for achieving a front-facing display. And those oversized pocket charts are also perfect for displaying magazines, web articles, or newspapers.

To maintain excitement for classroom book displays, change the arrangement of the texts frequently. To increase access to your classroom collection, rotate titles on the rain gutters in and out of your library shelves. To diversify your options, add titles from the school or public library, and swap texts with colleagues. Trading books with grade-level partners or teachers at other grade levels is a wonderful way to introduce books of varying genres or levels.

Classroom environment is an important element for engaged reading as noted in Section 2.

And last, use ongoing reviews to encourage interaction about nontraditional book displays. Slightly enlarged bookmarks can be made available to anyone (students, teachers, building principal, classroom visitors, etc.) who would like to write a review of a displayed text. Like any worthy book review, likes and dislikes should be specific enough to convey a well-reasoned opinion but not so detailed as to spoil an ending or ruin the reading for another. Providing a few examples of grade-appropriate reviews written by reading role models such as older peers, teachers, or the building principal is a sure way to jump-start the reviewing process. And do recall that opinions are sure to vary. Be prepared for and welcome the discussions as students are motivated to write and read reviews. There is nothing better than a passionate book debate among avid readers.

Bridging the Book Divide

In an effort to encourage reading at home, teachers and librarians often send books home. There is little doubt that such practices are important. However, let's stop for a moment and consider the absolutely unintentional message books in backpacks might send. Are we communicating that only the books sent home by teachers or librarians are "the best" or those that are "valued"? Is there the implicit message that school is the only place important books live?

While we never want to stop sending books home, a way to increase access and bridge the book divide is to invite books (and all print) shared at home into your classroom and library. As Figure 3–14 illustrates, such reciprocity encourages dialogue between home and school. The messaging from efforts to bridge the book divide are important. Teachers are communicating (without nagging) the expectation that reading occurs at home above and beyond the backpack books and that this sharing of print is valued. When the invitation to share home reading is extended, it is critical to stress that you are interested in whatever their child is enjoying (joke books, a favorite website, a magazine article, etc.), no matter where the print originated. Recognize that parents can surround their children with print. We believe every family has print to

Figure 3–14   Books from Andrew's Home

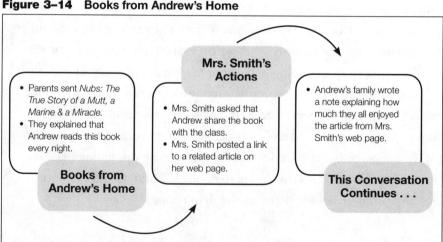

- Parents sent *Nubs: The True Story of a Mutt, a Marine & a Miracle*.
- They explained that Andrew reads this book every night.

Books from Andrew's Home

Mrs. Smith's Actions

- Mrs. Smith asked that Andrew share the book with the class.
- Mrs. Smith posted a link to a related article on her web page.

- Andrew's family wrote a note explaining how much they all enjoyed the article from Mrs. Smith's web page.

This Conversation Continues . . .

Figure 3–15   A Suggestion for Andrew's Family

To: JonesFamily@gmail.com

From: Smith@anywhereelementaryschool.org

Hello to the Jones family,

Andrew shared *Nubs: The True Story of a Mutt, a Marine, and a Miracle* by Brian Dennis and Mary Nethery with the class. They loved it! Thank you for sharing this wonderful book from your home! Did you know Nubs has his own web page? It can be found at:

http://www.hachettebookgroup.com/features/storyofnubs/index.html

Based on the book you sent to us, I have a feeling Andrew might also enjoy *Tuesday Tucks Me In: The Loyal Bond between a Soldier and His Service Dog* by Luis Carlos Montalván, Bret Witter, and Dan Dion. I saw it at the public library yesterday. It is featured in the nonfiction section. Hope you can check it out!

Mrs. Smith

share regardless of income. Remind parents that interesting reads can come from home, libraries, public libraries, a visit to a museum or zoo, a grandparent's bookshelf, or the grocery store.

In addition to nurturing home–school reading motivation, the benefits of bridging the book divide for teachers are endless. Imagine beginning a parent-teacher conference with a quick chat about a book from home? Hearing about what your students are enjoying at home can inform your backpack selections or help you make suggestions at school. Home reading can be celebrated at school by profiling family favorites on your website or teacher blog. And you can encourage more reading by emailing a personal suggestion based on family sharing. For example, after learning about one of Andrew's favorite books, you might send an email like the one in Figure 3–15.

Bridging the book divide by inviting home reads into classrooms is a win-win situation! Recognizing this important reciprocity nurtures intrinsic motivation in children, their families, and you. Inviting families to share what they are reading with their children welcomes everyone into your literacy community. And imagine how excited you will be when the evidence of home reading comes pouring in!

Representing Reading

The excitement of a book club is all about the discussion of a shared reading experience. However, book clubs aren't the only way to gather to chat about text. How often have you been in the library, in the bookstore, or on a plane and started talking with someone about a book he or she was reading? You may have read the same book, or another by the same author, or a book about a similar topic. An interesting way to capture this same magic is to purposefully place together children who have similar reading interests. Or, to stimulate discussions about a wide variety of genres or topics, arrange groups that have diverse reading interests. The sometimes-challenging aspect to facilitating such discussions is keeping up with what students are reading.

To help with this task, we can borrow a method from social psychology called *sociometry*. Sociometry is a methodology for tracking the energy vectors of interpersonal relationships in a group. It shows the patterns of how individuals associate with each other when acting as a group (Leung and Silberling 2006). A visual representation of such interpersonal energies is called a *sociogram*. Sociograms have long been to identify social status in classrooms. As such, they are now being used by insightful school psychologists and classroom teachers to combat bullying and loneliness (Melton 2014).

In addition to examining social structure in a classroom, sociograms can also be used to explore relationships with text. After sharing a teacher-created model of your recent reading, students can create sociograms to represent what they have been reading and how they enjoyed it (or not). These visual representations can provide important insights. For example, you might use reading sociograms when rearranging the desks in your classrooms. Wouldn't it be interesting to create small groups based on similar reading interests? Or you might

Figure 3–16 Mia's Sociogram

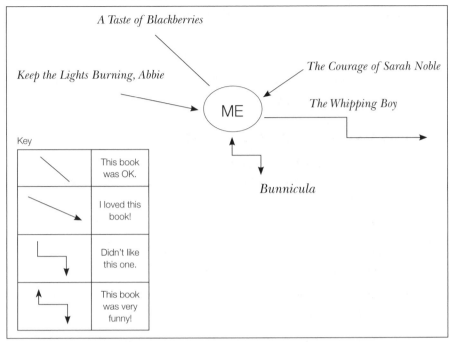

mix it up a bit, and seat together children who have very diverse tastes in texts. Their conversations could promote the sampling of new genres. Other uses for sociograms include informing book club or read-aloud selections as well as one-on-one reading concerns. For example, Figure 3–16 shows third grader Mia's sociogram. A quick look at her reading representation prompts questions. Would she enjoy other works of historical fiction? She likes some fantasy (*Bunnicula* [Howe 2006]) and not others (*The Whipping Boy* [Fleischman 2003]). Why? Does she not like all realistic fiction or just *Blackberries in the Dark*? Was it the death that disturbed her? Questions about Mia's sociogram could be discussed in a one-on-one reading conference, or patterns might become clear as she creates other sociograms. Thanks to our friends in the Greece Central School District, New York (2014) for offering some tips on conducting sociograms. Figure 3–17 contains their great ideas adapted for reading representations.

In order to afford as much choice as possible, consider doing socio-grams every few weeks. Interests change as children read widely and are exposed to a variety of print across the content areas. It is only by viewing several rounds of sociograms that patterns within and across readers/groups can be seen. Sociograms also make wonderful conversation starters during parent-teacher conferences.

Figure 3–17 **Tips for Creating Reading Sociograms**

- Remind students their reading sociograms should not be limited to just books. They should feel free to include articles, websites, poems, and so on.

- Place the child at the center of the diagram.

- Create a shared key together. Decide on the line shapes needed to present various reactions to reading.

- Let the size, shape, color, symbols, and line thickness metaphorically represent reactions.

- In addition to the line shapes presenting reactions, the physical distance of the lines can also be used to add emphasis. For example, a line from ME to a book I didn't like might be longer than a line from ME to a book I loved.

- Depending upon the age of your students, it is also possible to allow each child to create his or her own key. Do know, however, it is more time-consuming for the teacher to interpret sociograms that contain many different representations. And, if individual keys are created, remind children to keep them in a safe place for future use. To avoid confusion and frustration, keep individual keys consistent as students create multiple sociograms.

- Younger students can use pictures of characters and word cards to construct their sociograms.

- Software such as Inspiration can be used to help students create a sociogram.

Adapted from Central Greece School District 2014

Next Steps

> The measure of whether we are successful as literacy educators is whether individuals turn to texts for information, restoration, inspiration, and enjoyment. (Hiebert 2009, xii)

As teachers we are all on a journey to learn and develop insights about how to motivate our students to read. Creating a motivating classroom context for literacy learning requires thoughtful planning and knowledge about what does and does not result in intrinsic motivation. The joy we feel when we see our students reading for information, restoration, inspiration, and enjoyment makes the journey worthwhile. Wherever you are on your motivational journey, we hope that you will find the research and strategies we've shared with you to be of value and we wish you success in helping all your students develop the reading habit!

AFTERWORD

ELLIN OLIVER KEENE

You can't plan those moments: just a quick, but thought-provoking conversation with a colleague as you walk to the parking lot and linger next to your cars for a few minutes; the conversation with a literacy coach that changed your thinking about how to approach literacy learning in your own classroom; even the team meeting that led you to an engaging new way to get book clubs started in your classroom. These are *conversations,* not necessarily professional learning opportunities, aren't they? Often, the most transformative professional development isn't designated as such—it's just the right conversation at the right time.

I think you'll agree, now that you've finished this delicious book, that reading it was like sitting down with Barbara and Linda for a great conversation about truly engaging children in their own learning. As I read it, I felt like I was in a stimulating dialogue with them—the voice with which they write sounds so familiar and open, never judging, but acknowledging that we've all tried to woo kids into reading with extrinsic motivational tools, and we've all found that the outcomes are all too brief or actually work against our best intentions. Now it's time to ignite the conversation with your colleagues. How about sharing a quote or two from this book at the next grade-level meeting or when someone suggests that the principal take a pie in the face to "motivate" kids to read. Perhaps they have an ulterior motive by suggesting! How about posting a word or two about it on Twitter? How about sharing ways in which their immensely practical ideas have led to changes in your own classroom?

We humbly thank Barbara and Linda, who have engaged us in the kind of conversation about engagement that they and, as series editors, Nell and I fervently hope will lead to a widening circle of important conversations and many more readers for this book. We want all kids to be engaged as some are, and now we have a clear idea about what the research supports and exactly how we can approach them in the classroom.

REFERENCES

Professional Works Cited

Ainley, M., S. Hidi, and D. Berndorff. 2002. "Interest, Learning, and the Psychological Processes That Mediate Their Relationship." *Journal of Educational Psychology* 94 (3): 545–61.

Allington, R. L. 2011. "Reading Intervention in the Middle Grades." *Voices from the Middle* 19 (2): 10–16.

———. 2013. "What Really Matters When Working with Struggling Readers." *The Reading Teacher* 66 (7): 520–30.

Allington, R. L., R. E. Gabriel, and M. Billen. 2012. "Middle Schoolers and Magazines: What Teachers Can Learn from Students' Leisure Reading Habits." *The Clearing House* 85: 186–91.

Allington, R. L., and A. McGill-Franzen. 2003. "The Impact of Summer Loss on the Reading Achievement Gap." *Phi Delta Kappan* 85 (6): 68–75.

American Library Association. 2014. "Core Values." Retrieved from www.ala .org/advocacy/intfreedom/statementspols/corevalues#access.

Ames, C. A. 1992. "Classrooms: Goals, Structures, and Student Motivation." *Journal of Educational Psychology* 84: 261–71.

Anderman, E. M., and C. Midgley. 1992. "Changes in Achievement Goal Orientations, Perceived Academic Competence, and Grades Across the Transition to Middle-Level Schools." *Contemporary Educational Psychology* 22 (3): 269–98.

Bandura, A. 1977. *Social Learning Theory*. New York: General Learning Press.

Bauer, N. 2011. *Dog Heroes of September 11th: A Tribute to America's Search and Rescue Dogs*. New York: Kennel Club Books.

Brennan, T. P., and J. A. Glover. 1980. "An Examination of the Effect of Extrinsic Reinforcers on Intrinsically Motivated Behavior: Experimental and Theoretical." *Social Behavior and Personality* 8: 27–32.

Brenner, D., E. H. Hiebert, and R. Tompkins. 2010. "How Much and What Are Third Graders Reading? Reading in Core Programs." In *Reading More, Reading Better*, edited by E. H. Hiebert, 118–40. New York: Guilford Press.

Brophy, J. 2004. *Motivating Students to Learn*, 2nd ed. Mahwah, NJ: Erlbaum.

———. 2008. "Developing Students' Appreciation for What Is Taught in School." *Educational Psychologist* 43 (3): 132–41.

Brown, J. S., A. Collins, and P. Duguid. 1989. "Situated Cognition and the Culture of Learning." *Educational Researcher* 18: 32–42.

Cambourne, B. 1995 "Toward an Educationally Relevant Theory of Literacy Learning: Twenty Years of Inquiry." *The Reading Teacher* 49 (3): 182–90.

Cameron, J., and W. D. Pierce. 1994. "Reinforcement, Reward, and Intrinsic Motivation: A Meta-Analysis." *Review of Educational Research* 64: 363–423.

Christensen, P., and A. James, eds. 2008. *Research with Children: Perspectives and Practices*. New York: Routledge.

Clark, A., and P. Moss. 2011. *Listening to Young Children: The Mosaic Approach*. Philadelphia: Jessica Kingsley Publishers.

Coley, J. D. 1981. "Nonstop Reading for Teenagers: What We Have Learned and Where We Go from Here." Paper presented at the annual meeting of the College Reading Association, Louisville, KY. (ERIC Document Reproduction Service No. ED 211951.)

Common Core Standards Initiative. 2012. Common Core State Standards for English Language Arts & Literacy in History/Social Studies, Science, and Technical Subjects. Retrieved from www.corestandards.org/.

Condon, M. 2014. "The Formative Assessment Question Everyone Should Ask." Retrieved from http://about.uniteforliteracy.com/blog/page/3/.

Csikszentmihalyi, M. 1990. *Flow: The Psychology of Optimal Experience*. New York: Harper & Row.

———. 1991. *Flow: The Psychology of Optimal Experience*, vol. 41. New York: HarperPerennial.

Cunningham, A. E., and K. E. Stanovich. 1998. "What Reading Does for the Mind." *American Educator* (spring/summer): 8–15.

Deci, E. L. 1975. *Intrinsic Motivation*. New York: Plenum.

Deci, E. L., and R. M. Ryan. 1985. *Intrinsic Motivation and Self-Determination in Human Behavior*. New York: Plenum.

Deci, E. L., R. M. Valerand, L. Pelletier, and R. Ryan. 1991. "Motivation and Education: The Self-Determination Perspective." *Educational Psychologist* 26: 325–47.

Duke, N. K., V. Purcell-Gates, L. A. Hall, and C. Tower. 2006. "Authentic Literacy Activities for Developing Comprehension and Writing." *The Reading Teacher* 60 (4): 344–55.

Dweck, C. S., and E. L. Leggett. 1988. "A Social-Cognitive Approach to Motivation and Personality." *Psychological Review* 95: 256–73.

Eccles, J., T. Adler, R. Futterman, S. B. Goff, C. M. Kaezala, J. L. Meece, et al. 1983. "Expectancies, Values, and Academic Behaviors." In *Achievement and Achievement Motives: Psychological and Sociological Approaches*, edited by J. T. Spence, 75–146. San Francisco: Freeman.

Foorman, B. R., C. Schatschneider, M. N. Eakin, J. M. Fletcher, L. C. Moats, and D. J. Francis. 2006. "The Impact of Instructional Practices in Grades 1 and 2 on Reading and Spelling Achievement in High Poverty Schools." *Contemporary Educational Psychology* 31: 1–29.

Fryer, R., S. Levitt, J. List, and S. Sadoff. 2012. *Enhancing the Efficacy of Teacher Incentives Through Loss Aversion: A Field Experiment*. Washington, DC: National Bureau of Economic Research. NBER Working Paper No. 18237.

Fulmer, S. M. and J. C. Frijters. 2011. "Motivation During an Excessively Challenging Reading Task: The Buffering Role of Relative Topic Interest." *Journal of Experimental Education* 79: 185–208.

Ga'Hoole wiki. Owl terminology. Retrieved at http://guardiansofgahoole .wikia.com/wiki/Owl_Terminology.

Gambrell, L. B. 1996. "Creating Classroom Cultures That Foster Reading Motivation." *Reading Teacher* 50: 14–25.

———. 2011. "Seven Rules of Engagement: What's Most Important to Know About Motivation to Read." *The Reading Teacher* 65 (3): 172–78.

Gambrell, L. B., E. Hughes, W. Calvert, J. Malloy, and B. Igo. 2011. "Authentic Reading, Writing, and Discussion: An Exploratory Study of a Pen Pal Project." *Elementary School Journal* 112 (2): 234–58.

Gambrell, L. B., and B. A. Marinak. 1997. "Incentives and Intrinsic Motivation to Read." In *Reading Engagement: Motivating Readers Through Integrated Instruction*, edited by J. T. Guthrie and A. Wigfield, 205–17. Newark, DE: International Reading Association.

Gambrell, L.B., and B. A. Marinak. 2014. "Simple Practices to Nurture the Motivation to Read." Reading Rockets. Retrieved from http://www.reading rockets.org/article/simple-practices-nurture-motivation-read.

Gavelek, J. R., and T. E. Raphael. 1996. "Changing Talk About Text: New Roles for Teachers and Students." *Language Arts* 73 (3): 182–92.

Greece Central School District. 2014. *Sociograms*. Retrieved from http://www
.greececsd.org/academics.cfm?subpage=1249.

Green, S. S. 1876. "Personal Relations Between Librarians and Readers."
Library Journal 1 (2): 74–81.

Guthrie, J. T. 2011. "Best Practices in Motivating Students to Read." In *Best
Practices in Literacy Instruction*, 177–98. New York: Guilford Press.

Guthrie, J. T., and N. M. Humenick. 2004. "Motivating Students to
Read: Evidence for Classroom Practices That Increase Motivation and
Achievement." In *The Voice of Evidence in Reading Research*, edited by P.
McCardle and V. Chabra, 329–54. Baltimore: Brookes.

Guthrie, J. T., and A. D. McCann. 1997. "Characteristics of Classrooms That
Promote Motivations and Strategies for Learning." In *Reading Engagement:
Motivating Readers Through Integrated Instruction*, edited by J. T. Guthrie and A.
Wigfield, 128–48. Newark, DE: International Reading Association.

Guthrie, J. T., A. McRae, and S. L. Klauda. 2007. "Contributions of Concept-
Oriented Reading Instruction to Knowledge About Interventions for
Motivations in Reading." *Educational Psychologist* 42 (4): 237–50.

Guthrie, J. T., A. Wigfield, J. L. Metsala, and K. E. Cox. 1999. "Motivational
and Cognitive Predictors of Text Comprehension and Reading Amount."
Scientific Studies of Reading 3 (3): 231–56.

Guthrie, J. T., A. Wigfield, and C. VonSecker. 2000. "Effects of Integrated
Instruction on Motivation and Strategy Use in Reading." *Journal of
Educational Psychology* 92 (2): 331–41.

Head, M. H., and J. E. Readence. 1986. "Anticipation Guides: Enhancing
Meaning Through Prediction." In *Reading in the Content Areas: Improving
Classroom Instruction*, 2nd ed., edited by E. K. Dishner, T. W. Bean, and J. E.
Readence, 229–34. Dubuque, IA: Kendall/Hunt.

Hohmann, M., D. P. Weikart, and A. S. Epstein. 1995. *Educating Young
Children: Active Learning Practices for Preschool and Child Care Programs*.
Ypsilanti, MI: High/Scope Press.

Hidi, S. 1990. "Interest and Its Contribution as a Mental Resource for
Learning." *Review of Educational Research* 60 (4): 549–71.

Hidi, S., and J. M. Harackiewicz. 2000. "Motivating the Academically
Unmotivated: A Critical Issue for the 21st Century." *Review of Educational
Research* 70 (2): 151–79.

Hiebert, E. H., ed. 2009. *Reading More, Reading Better*. New York: Guilford Press.

Jang, H., J. Reeve, and E. L. Deci. 2010. "Engaging Students in Learning Activities: It Is Not Autonomy Support or Structure but Autonomy Support and Structure." *Journal of Educational Psychology* 102: 588–600.

Karnoil, R., and M. Ross. 1977. "The Effect of Performance Relevant and Performance Irrelevant Rewards on Children's Intrinsic Motivation." *Child Development* 48: 482–87.

Krapp, A., S. Hidi, and A. Renninger. 1992. "Interest, Learning, and Development." In *The Role of Interest in Learning and Development*, edited by R. A. Renninger, S. Hidi, and A. Krapp, 3–25. Hillsdale, NJ: Erlbaum.

Krashen, S. 2005. "Accelerated Reader: Evidence Still Lacking." *Knowledge Quest* 33 (3): 48–49.

Lapp, D., J. Flood, C. H. Brock, and D. Fisher. 2013. *Teaching Reading to Every Child*. New York: Routledge.

Lepper, M. R., D. Greene, and R. E. Nisbett. 1973. "Undermining Children's Intrinsic Interest with Extrinsic Reward." *Journal of Personality and Social Psychology* 28: 124–37.

Leung, B. P., and J. Silberling. 2006. "Using Sociograms to Identify Social Status in the Classroom." *The California School Psychologist* 11 (1): 57–61.

Mallette, M. H., W. A. Henk, and S. A. Melnick. 2004. "The Influence of Accelerated Reader on the Affective Literacy Orientations of Intermediate Grade Students." *Journal of Literacy Research* 36 (1): 73–84.

Marinak, B., and L. Gambrell. 2008. "Intrinsic Motivation and Rewards: What Sustains Young Children's Engagement with Text?" *Literacy Research and Instruction* 47 (1): 9–26.

———. 2009. "Developmental Differences in Elementary Reading Motivation." Paper presented at the annual meeting of the Association of Literacy Educators and Researchers, Charlotte, NC.

Marinak, B. A., L. B. Gambrell, and J. A. Malloy. 2013. "I Read Only Dog Books! Engaged Reading for Students on the Autistic Spectrum." In *Struggling Readers Can Succeed: Teaching Solutions Based on Real Kids in Classrooms and Communities*, edited by N. Nilsson and D. Gandy, 89–109. Charlotte, NC: Information Age Publishing.

Marinak, B., L. Gambrell, and S. Mazzoni. 2012. *Maximizing Motivation in Literacy Classrooms, K–6*. New York: Guilford Press.

Marinak, B., M. Strickland, and J. Keat. 2010. "A Mosaic of Words: Using Photo Narration to Support All Learners." *Young Children* 65 (5): 32–38.

Mayes, F. J. 1982. "U.S.S.R. for Poor Readers." *Orbit* 13: 3–4.

McKenna, M. C. 2001. "Development of Reading Attitudes." In *Literacy and Motivation: Reading Engagement in Individuals and Groups,* edited by L. Verhoeven and C. Snow, 135–58. Mahwah, NJ: Erlbaum.

McKenna, M. C., K. Conradi, C. Lawrence, B. G. Jang, and J. P. Meyer. 2012. "Reading Attitudes of Middle School Students: Results of a U.S. Survey." *Reading Research Quarterly* 47 (3): 283–305.

McKenna, M. C., D. J. Kear, and R. A. Ellsworth. 1995. "Children's Attitudes Toward Reading: A National Survey." *Reading Research Quarterly* 30 (4): 934–56.

Melton, G. 2014. *Share This with All Schools Please.* Retrieved from http://momastery.com/blog/2014/01/30/share-schools/.

Miller, D., and B. Moss. 2013. *No More Independent Reading Without Support.* Portsmouth, NH: Heinemann.

Mizelle, N. B. 1997. "Enhancing Young Adolescents' Motivation for Literacy Learning." *Middle School Journal* 24 (2): 5–14.

Morrow, L. M. 1982. "Relationships Between Literature Programs, Library Corner Designs, and Children's Use of Literature." *Journal of Educational Research* 75: 339–44.

———. 1990. "Preparing the Classroom Environment to Promote Literacy During Play." *Early Childhood Research Quarterly* 5: 537–54.

Morrow, L. M., K. A. Roskos, and L. B. Gambrell. 2015. *Oral Language and Comprehension in Preschool: Teaching the Essentials.* New York: Guilford.

Moss, B. and T. A. Young. 2010. *Creating Lifelong Readers Through Independent Reading.* Newark, DE: International Reading Association.

Neuman, S. B., and D. Celano. 2001. "Access to Print in Low-Income and Middle-Income Communities: An Ecological Study of Four Neighborhoods." *Reading Research Quarterly* 36 (1): 8–26.

Neuman, S. B., and K. Roskos. 1997. "Literacy Knowledge in Practice: Contexts of Participation for Young Writers and Readers." *Reading Research Quarterly* 32: 10–32.

Niegaard, H. 1994. "UNESCO's 1994 Public Library Manifesto." In *Proceedings of the 60th IFLA Council and General Conference,* Havana, August 23. www.ifla.org/publications/iflaunesco-public-library-manifesto-1994.

Ng, M. M., J. T. Guthrie, P. Van Meter, A. McCann, and S. Alao. 1998. "How Classroom Characteristics Influence Intrinsic Motivations for Literacy." *Reading Psychology* 19: 319–98.

Palmer, B. M., R. M. Codling, and L. B. Gambrell. 1994. "In Their Own Words: What Elementary Children Have to Say About Motivation to Read." *The Reading Teacher* 48: 176–79.

Paris, S. G., and E. R. Oka. 1986. "Strategies for Comprehending Text and Coping with Reading Difficulties." *Learning Disability Quarterly* 12 (1): 32–42.

Patall, E. A., H. Cooper, and S. R. Wynn. 2010. "The Effectiveness and Relative Importance of Choice in the Classroom." *Journal of Educational Psychology* 102: 896–915.

Perks, K. 2010. "Crafting Effective Choices to Motivate Students. *Adolescent Literacy in Perspective* (March/April): 2–3. Available at www.ohiorc.org/orc _documents/ORC/Adlit/InPerspective/2010-03/in_perspective_2010-03.pdf.

Petscher, Y. 2010. "A Meta-Analysis of the Relationship Between Student Attitudes Towards Reading and Achievement in Reading." *Journal of Research in Reading* 33 (4): 335–55.

Pressley, M. 1989. "Strategies That Improve Children's Memory and Comprehension of Text." *The Elementary School Journal* 90: 3–12.

———. 1997. "The Cognitive Science of Reading." *Contemporary Educational Psychology* 22 (2): 247–59.

———. 2007. "Achieving Best Practices." In *Best Practices in Literacy Instruction*, edited by L. B. Gambrell, L. M. Morrow, and M. Pressley, 397–404. New York: Guilford Press.

Purcell-Gates, V. 1996. "What Does Culture Have to Do with It?" In *55th Yearbook of the National Reading Conference*, edited by J. V. Hoffman, D. L. Schallert, C. M. Fairbanks, J. Worthy, and B. Maloch, 43–59. Oak Creek, WI: NRC.

———. 2002. "Authentic Literacy in Class Yields Increase in Literacy Practices." *Literacy Update* 11: 7.

Purcell-Gates, V., N. K. Duke, and J. A. Martineau. 2007. "Learning to Read and Write Genre-Specific Text: Roles of Authentic Experience and Explicit Teaching." *Reading Research Quarterly* 42 (1): 8–45.

Raphael, T. E., S. Florio-Ruane, and M. George. 2001. "Book Club 'Plus': A Conceptual Framework to Organize Literacy Instruction." *Language Arts*: 159–68.

Rettig, M. K., and C. G. Hendricks. 2000. "Factors That Influence the Book Selection Process of Students with Special Needs." *Journal of Adolescent & Adult Literacy* 43 (7): 608–18.

Reynolds, P. L., and S. Symons. 2001. "Motivational Variables and Children's Text Search." *Journal of Educational Psychology* 93: 14.

Rotter, J. B. 1966. "Generalized Expectancies for Internal Versus External Control of Reinforcement." *Psychological Monographs: General and Applied* 80 (1): 1–28.

Schiefele, U. 1991. "Interest, Learning, and Motivation." *Educational Psychologist* 26 (3–4): 299–323.

Schunk, D. H. 1989. "Social Cognitive Theory and Self-Regulated Learning." In *Self-Regulated Learning and Academic Achievement*, edited by B. J. Zimmerman and D. H. Schunk, 83–110. New York: Springer-Verlag.

Schunk, D., P. Pintrich, and J. Meece. 2008. *Motivation in Education: Theory, Research, and Application*. New York: Pearson.

Schunk, D. H., and B. J. Zimmerman. 1997. "Developing Self-Efficacious Readers and Writers: The Role of Social and Self-Regulatory Processes." In *Reading Engagement: Motivating Readers Through Integrated Instruction*, edited by J. T. Guthrie and A. Wigfield, 34–50. Newark, DE: International Reading Association.

Schmidt, R. 2008. "Really Reading: What Does Accelerated Reader Teach Adults and Children?" *Language Arts*: 202–11.

Skinner, E. A., and M. J. Belmont. 1993. "Motivation in the Classroom: Reciprocal Effects of Teacher Behavior and Students Engagement Across the School Year." *Journal of Educational Psychology* 85: 571–81.

Skinner, B. F. 1953. *Science and Human Behavior.* New York: Free Press.

Spaulding, C. L. 1992. *Motivation in the Classroom.* New York: McGraw-Hill.

Stine, R. L. 1992–1997. *Goosebumps*, original series. New York: Scholastic.

Stipek, D. J. 2002. *Motivation to Learn: Integrating Theory and Practice.* Allyn & Bacon.

Taylor, B. M., B. J. Frye, and G. M. Maruyama. 1990. "Time Spent Reading and Reading Growth." *American Educational Research Journal* 27(2): 351–62.

Thorndike, E. L. 1910. "The Contribution of Psychology to Education." *Journal of Educational Psychology* 1: 5–12.

Tobias, S. 1994. "Interest, Prior Knowledge, and Learning." *Review of Educational Research* 64 (1): 37–54.

Trelease, J. 2015. "Rain Gutter Revolution." Retrieved from http://tprsteacher .com/activities/reading/rain-gutter-bookshelves/.

Turner, J. 1995. "The Influence of Classroom Contexts on Young Children's Motivation for Literacy." *Reading Research Quarterly* 30 (3): 410–41.

Turner, J., and S. G. Paris. 1995. "How Literacy Tasks Influence Children's Motivation for Literacy." *The Reading Teacher* 48 (8): 662–73.

Voltaire. 2014. Retrieved from www.quotationspage.com/quotes/Voltaire.

Watson, J. B. 1913. "Psychology as the Behaviorist Views It." *Psychological Review* 20: 158–77.

Wayne, A. J., and P. Youngs. 2003. "Teacher Characteristics and Student Achievement Gains: A Review." *Review of Educational Research* 73 (1): 89–122.

Whitehead, N. 2004. "The Effects of Increased Access to Books on Student Reading Using the Public Library." *Reading Improvement* 41 (3): 165.

Wiesendanger, K. D., and E. D. Birlem. 1984. "The Effectiveness of SSR: An Overview of the Research." *Reading Horizons* 24 (3): 197–201.

Wigfield, A., and J. T. Guthrie. 1995. *Dimension of Children's Motivations for Reading: An Initial Study* (Research Report no. 34). Athens, GA: National Reading Research Center.

———. 2000. "Engagement and Motivation in Reading." *Handbook of Reading Research* 3: 403–22.

Wikia. 2014. *Yarping*. Retrieved from www.wikia.com/Wikia.

Worthy, J., E. Patterson, R. Salas, S. Prater, and M. Turner. 2001. "'More Than Just Reading': The Human Factor in Reaching Resistant Readers." *Literacy Research and Instruction* 41 (2): 177–201.

Wu, Y., and S. J. Samuels. 2004. "How the Amount of Time Spent on Independent Reading Affects Reading Achievement: A Response to the National Reading Panel." Paper presented at the International Reading Association 49th Annual Convention, Reno, Nevada.

Children's Literature Cited

Dennis, B., and M. Nethery. 2009. *Nubs: The True Story of a Mutt, a Marine, and a Miracle*. New York: Little, Brown Books for Young Readers.

Fitzhugh, L. 1994. *Harriet the Spy*. New York: HarperTrophy.

Florian, D. 2007. *Comets, Stars, the Moon, and Mars: Space Poems and Paintings*. New York: HMH Books for Young Readers.

Fleischman, S. 2003. *The Whipping Boy*. New York: Greenwillow Books.

Howe, J. 2006. *Bunnicula*. New York: Great Source.

Howe, J. 2000. *Dew Drop Dead*. New York: Atheneum Books for Young Readers.

Lasky, K. 2003. *The Guardians of Ga'Hoole*. New York: Scholastic.

Montalván, L. C., B. Witter, and D. Dion. 2014. *Tuesday Tucks Me In: The Loyal Bond Between a Soldier and His Service Dog*. New York: Roaring Book Press.

Sattler, H. 1998. *The Book of North American Owls*. New York: HMH Books for Young Readers.

Simon, S. 2007. *Snakes*. New York. HarperCollins.

Smithsonian. 2013. *Everything You Need to Know About Snakes*. New York: DK Publishing.

White, M. 2012. *National Geographic Angry Birds: 50 True Stories of the Fed Up, Feathered, and Furious*. New York. National Geographic.